ALL KINDS OF KINGS
IN FACT AND LEGEND
From Hammurabi to Louis XIV

Johanna Johnston
and
Murry Karmiller

From Hammurabi to Louis XIV

W·W·NORTON & COMPANY·INC·New York

Contents

A Note from the Authors

Kings have always fascinated people. Nowadays we may not regard them with the same awe and terror that people once did, but kings always stand above the crowd, the focus of attention whenever they appear—inspiring envy, curiosity and excitement.

Because of their position, every quality of their characters becomes magnified. In the past, when kings were all-powerful and shaped the destiny of nations, if a king was good, he seemed very, very good. If he was bad, he seemed terrible. The virtues and vices of all mankind seemed to be represented on a grand scale in kings. This makes them wonderfully entertaining and dramatic to read about—however awe-inspiring they may have been in life.

This book tells stories of—and legends about—some of the best-known of the world's kings, from one of the very earliest who lived four thousand years ago, to one who ruled in splendor and absolute authority only three hundred years in the past. The tales about them that have made them household names are recalled and historical facts about each king are also given. His country and his times are described and the things he did that made him famous—or infamous.

"Live forever, O King," is a phrase people used to use to flatter a king. And the kings in this book do seem to live on and on—the name of each one almost a shorthand symbol for bravery or wickedness, wisdom, wealth, nobility, or greed.

JOHANNA JOHNSTON AND
MURRY KARMILLER

PART ONE

CONQUERING KINGS

See the conquering hero comes!
  Sound the trumpet, beat the drums!
    Joshua, DR. THOMAS MORELL (1703–1784)

Alexander the Great

Mithridates

Harold Fairhair

William the Conqueror

Richard the Lionhearted

1

Alexander the Great

ALEXANDER was the great conqueror of the ancient world. He conquered not only the countries that were known to the Greeks and their neighbors but marched his armies so far eastward into lands that were unknown that it seemed as if he had marched across and conquered all the world. Young and handsome, with dreams of uniting the many lands that he conquered into one large world-state, he was a dazzling hero not only in his own time but has remained one through the ages.

Alexander's Parents and Homeland

Alexander was born in 356 B.C., in Macedonia, a large, rough, hilly country north of Greece. He was the son of King Philip and his wife, Olympias.

King Philip was a conqueror himself. He had marched against the barbaric tribes to the north and east of Macedonia and conquered them. He had marched southward into Greece and managed, both by fighting and persuasion, to become the military leader of the previously independent Greek city-states. Philip had lost an eye and become crippled in the course of this fighting but he still had plans for more conquest. He wanted to take his armies to the east coast of the Mediterranean and recapture the Greek city-states there from the rule of Darius III, the great king of Persia. But in 336 B.C., before he could start on this expedition, he was assassinated. His son, Alexander, became king of Macedonia at twenty years of age.

His March of Conquest

Alexander at once began to carry out his father's plans. He readied the army, arranged for supplies, and then marched his troops eastward and

southward (past Troy, which had been the scene of the Trojan War, many years before) , down the eastern coast of the Mediterranean.

Soon he was challenged by King Darius and some of his Persian host. But Alexander and his men defeated the Persians easily, and Darius fled in his chariot, leaving his family behind. Alexander treated these hostages kindly and took them with him as he marched on, through the land that is now Israel.

He came to the island city of Tyre, laid siege to it, and finally forced it to surrender. He went on through the land of the Arabs into Egypt, and in Memphis he was acclaimed as Egypt's ruler, or Pharaoh.

From Egypt he turned eastward and northward again and traveled to the interior of Asia Minor and the Tigris-Euphrates valley. The Persian king, Darius, again challenged him. Again Alexander defeated Darius and his armies.

Eastward to Babylon, the garden city of the ancient kings, farther yet to Persepolis, capital of the Persian Empire, then still farther, into lands that no Macedonians or Greeks had ever visited before—Alexander kept his army marching on. He was exploring as well as conquering now, traveling over deserts and mountains, skirting the Caspian Sea, finally entering what is now southern Russia. Then Alexander turned southward and led his army across Afghanistan and Pakistan into India.

Alexander and his army were three thousand miles in a straight line from Macedonia, but the route they had followed had taken them eight or nine thousand miles. Across all those miles the people now acknowledged Alexander as their king, their overlord, their emperor. Whatever their highest title was, they gave it to him.

Alexander's Treatment of His Subjects

Alexander was rarely harsh with the people he conquered. Instead, he tried to organize the government of each country so as to preserve the best of what already existed while adding what was best and most appropriate from Greek civilization. He wanted a united world, where all sorts of different people could think, work, and worship as they chose while still being part of one world-state.

To hasten this feeling of relationship, he encouraged his soldiers to marry the women in the countries he conquered. He himself married an Oriental woman.

He founded cities wherever he went to serve as models. Seventy cities named Alexandria were established, among them today's thriving city of Alexandria in Egypt.

Alexander's Death

For eight years Alexander marched, conquered, and explored farther and farther to the east. Through the years some of his men were killed in battle, some settled in the cities he founded, some returned home. But all the while fresh troops were arriving, finding their way to him wherever he might be. Then, after lingering several months in India, Alexander decided to turn his men on the homeward way.

His navy sailed westward through the Indian Ocean and the Persian Gulf. His army followed along the coast. The journey was not hurried. Three years after the departure from India Alexander and the army had traveled only as far as Babylon, half way home to Macedonia.

In Babylon, Alexander became ill with some sort of fever. Before anyone realized how sick he was, he was dead. It was 323 B.C. He was thirty-three years old. This great general was also one of the most romantic figures of history. He was one of the few kings whose deeds were as startling as the many legends which later grew up around his exploits.

The End of Alexander's Empire

Alexander's only child, a son, was not born until after Alexander's death. The immense empire Alexander had created had to be ruled by his generals and closest friends. Gradually they began to quarrel among themselves, fighting with each other until the greatest empire the world had ever known fell apart.

Alexander's idea of a world-state, however, did not quite die. After Alexander was gone, people of different lands still knew about each other as they had not before. Greek ideas and customs that Alexander had introduced in the East left their mark on civilization there.

Legends about Alexander

Legends sprang up about Alexander while he was still alive. People said that he was not the son of Philip of Macedonia but that Zeus, king of the gods, had been his father. They said that on the night that Alexander was born the air changed color, thunder and lightning shook the earth, and animals trembled, knowing that a child was being born who would rule all things.

Strange tales were told about his mother, Olympias. She was a wild and passionate woman and, before marrying Philip, had been a priestess in her own country of Epirus, west of Greece. Taming and training great serpents had been part of her religious duties. People pictured Olympias with snakes twined about her arms and shoulders and other serpents coiled in the latticework of her bedroom.

Alexander's Horse, Bucephalus

One famous story about Alexander told of how he got his horse. He was still a boy and out in the fields one day, watching as some of his father's men inspected a new group of colts for the royal stables. Alexander noticed one big black colt with a white blaze on his forehead like an ox. Alexander thought that this oxheaded black animal was the best of the lot. But the colt kicked and bucked when the inspectors tried to put him through his paces. Soon they called a handler to take him away.

Alexander ran to his father. "Oh, please," he said, "that colt with the head like an ox—he's the best of all. The men do not know how to handle him."

King Philip turned to look at his son. "You think my handlers do not know how to manage horses?"

Alexander persisted. "I know what is wrong. I could manage him. I could ride him around the course and hold him to the rein."

The men standing around his father laughed. One said, "If you try—and fail?"

"I'll wager the price of the colt that I can do it," said Alexander.

"I do not know where you will get such a sum of money," said King Philip. "However, you made your wager. Go see what you can do with the colt. And if you *do* ride him, I will buy him for you."

Alexander ran out into the field, but as he approached the colt he began to walk slowly. He took the reins from the handler and spoke softly to the animal. Then he began turning the colt's head toward the sun. The colt grew calmer. Soon he was bending his head to nibble some grass.

Alexander jumped lightly onto his back. The colt stiffened and leaped forward, but Alexander stayed on, still holding the reins to keep the animal's eyes toward the sun. The colt began to gallop, and Alexander kept his seat.

They came to the oval runway. Alexander pulled the reins to turn the colt onto the course. For a moment, the colt strained. Then he settled down to an even gallop around the track.

When Alexander arrived in front of his father he checked the colt, slipped from his back, and patted his flank.

"How did you do it?" asked Philip.

"All I did was notice that at this hour the sun casts very long, black shadows," said Alexander. "When the inspectors were handling Oxhead they had him turned so that he faced the shadows. He was frightened by the dark, twisting shapes. I turned his head to the sun so that there was nothing to frighten him. You saw how he behaved then."

Philip turned to one of the men around him. "You may take the money from the treasury to buy the colt for Alexander," he said.

And that was how Alexander won the horse he named Bucephalus, which is Greek for oxhead, the horse that he would ride a quarter of the way around the world, in later years.

Alexander's Teacher, Aristotle

No king's son in history ever had a teacher as remarkable as the one Alexander had. His father hired as his tutor one of the greatest thinkers the world has ever known, the philosopher Aristotle. Aristotle had been born in Macedonia. Then, as a young man he traveled to Athens where he studied under the philosopher Plato. Philip brought Aristotle back to Macedonia to set up a school for Alexander and a few sons of Macedonian noblemen.

Aristotle assigned scientific projects to the boys, so Alexander spent many hours collecting, examining, and classifying rocks, fish, insects, and birds. Sometimes Aristotle walked among the boys as they worked and asked them questions to sharpen their reasoning powers.

"Suppose you were alone in a small boat far out at sea when a storm blew up. What would you do?" he asked one day.

The boys gave a variety of answers. One said he would drop sails and put out an anchor; another said he would make sacrifices to Poseidon, the god of the sea. Then it was Alexander's turn.

"What would you do, Alexander?" asked Aristotle.

"How can I know what I would do until the thing happened?" Alexander responded.

"It is an honest answer, at least," said Aristotle.

The answer also gave a hint about the kind of conqueror Alexander would become—a leader who did not waste time fearfully imagining what he might do in some future situation but pressed toward his goal trusting to inspiration to meet difficulties.

Alexander learned from Aristotle the most advanced ideas of the time about geography. The philosopher told his students that the earth was a sphere, hanging fixed in space, and that the sun, moon, and stars revolved around it. He told them that the northern part, or top of the sphere, was too cold to support life. The southern part, or bottom, was too hot. Only a belt of land running east and west part way around the globe was inhabitable. Greece and Macedonia were almost in the center of that inhabitable strip. The Pillars of Hercules, known today as the Strait of Gibraltar, marked the western end of the inhabitable lands and beyond, to the west, there was only ocean. The regions far to the east, beyond the lands bordering the Mediterranean Sea, were also a mystery. Men had traveled through the Dardanelles into a sea they called the Euxine, which is known today as the Black Sea. They had seen high mountains in the distance but had not traveled to them. Russia, China, and India were unknown to them. Hearing about those distant mountains far to the east, Alexander first began to dream of traveling into those unknown regions.

His later efforts to create a world-state were also inspired by Aristotle, for the philosopher spent many hours with the boys discussing the different ways men governed themselves. Under Aristotle's guidance, Alexander compared all kinds of political organizations from the most primitive to the most civilized and began pondering on what sort of government helped men to the happiest, most productive lives.

Natural science, geography, history, government—all these were studied by a most unusual boy with the world's greatest thinker for a teacher. No wonder that his ideas, when he set forth on his conquests, were somewhat unusual too.

Alexander and Famous Men

Alexander's story is studded with the names of famous men. Demosthenes, the greatest orator in Greece, had spoken and written against Alexander's father when Philip was trying to win leadership in Greece. Later, after Alexander's conquests, Demosthenes again tried to rally the Athenians to fight against Macedonian rule. But Macedonian soldiers threatened him. Demosthenes fled from them and later committed suicide.

Diogenes was another great name of the time. He was a Cynic philosopher and believed that men should care nothing about luxuries and possessions. One of the stories about Diogenes told of how he had walked through the streets of Athens at night carrying a lantern. Asked what he was doing, he replied, "I am looking for an honest man."

Alexander met Diogenes only once. He and some companions were walking along a road in Greece one day. They saw a man in a threadbare tunic resting in the sunshine by a large rock. Alexander's friends told him that the man was Diogenes.

Alexander walked over to the philosopher. Diogenes opened his eyes and looked at the young man who was the conqueror of Greece.

Alexander spoke humbly to the famous philosopher. "Is there anything I can do for you?" he asked.

"Yes," said Diogenes. "You can stand out of the sun."

(It is interesting that the sun and the shadows it casts figure in two stories about Alexander, who won fame by marching east, into the sun.)

Ptolemy is another name that echoes down the centuries because one Ptolemy after another was Pharaoh of Egypt.

The first Ptolemy was born in Macedonia. He was a schoolmate of Alexander's at Aristotle's academy and a trusted friend and captain at Alexander's side through all of Alexander's conquests. After Alexander's death, when the empire was divided, Ptolemy took over the administration of Egypt. He helped to make the city of Alexandria the great center of wealth and education that it became and he was the founder of Egypt's Ptolemaic dynasty.

Alexander and the Gordian Knot

In an inland city in Asia Minor called Gordium, an ancient wagon was enshrined in a temple. The wagon had been driven to the area many years before by the man who founded the city, and so it was cherished as a holy object. There was also a prophecy connected with it. The wagon shaft and yoke were roped together and held by a curious knot, so tied that the ends of the rope could not be seen. No one could figure out how to untie the knot. As a result, the prophecy was that when someone came along who could untie the Gordian knot that person was destined to be the Great King of Asia.

When Alexander went to Gordium in the first stages of his march through Asia Minor he went with some companions to look at the wagon and the knot. The more he looked, the more impossible it seemed to find a way to untie it. But Alexander would not admit defeat.

Later, one story said that he lifted his sword and cut the knot and so ended the difficulty. Another story said that he simply removed the wooden peg that joined the wagon shaft and the yoke and that when the yoke was free the knot untied itself. However it happened exactly, Alexander put an end to the puzzle of the Gordian knot, and everyone hailed him as the man destined to be the Great King.

Alexander the Mystic

Alexander was a man of action, but he was also a dreamer and visionary. He read Homer's poems when he was a boy and carried a copy of the *Iliad* with him through all his campaigning. He liked to think that the old Greek heroes, Hercules and Achilles, were his ancestors.

Cruelty, especially the cruelty of kings and warriors, was taken for granted by most people in his time. On occasion, Alexander was cruel. He destroyed the Greek city of Thebes to make the Greeks fear and respect him. He was merciless to the island city of Tyre, which resisted him for months. After hearing that one of his closest friends had made some critical remarks about him, he had his friend killed.

But Alexander was unusual in the remorse he suffered after such acts. Few kings ever thought they could do anything wrong. Alexander brooded about right and wrong and was unhappy when he felt he had erred.

And most unusual of all, of course, for a conqueror, was his belief that all people shared a common humanity and that the best aspects of the world's differing civilizations could be shared.

Alexander and Art

Alexander and his men carried a great deal of Greek art with them as they traveled into Asia Minor, Persia, and India. They had with them statues of their gods. Their weapons and clothing bore Greek decorations and designs. And all the cities Alexander built along his line of march had buildings in the Greek style of architecture.

Those Grecian objects and designs made a deep impression on the artists in the eastern countries, and from Alexander's time on, eastern art showed the influence of Greek art. In Asia, the god Buddha had never been represented in painting or sculpture until after the Buddhists saw Grecian statues. Then they began to portray a Buddha very like the Grecian Apollo.

The art on coins was also influenced by Alexander's conquests. His profile was the first portrait of a real person to be used on coins.

Alexander as a God

Many of Alexander's countrymen who knew only that their king marched farther into the unknown every year thought of him as a madman, insane with ambition to conquer the world.

In the meantime, many people in the countries through which he passed began worshiping him as a god. In Egypt, he was considered divine and given divine honors.

Long after Alexander's death, the Israelite people remembered him and linked him with the descendants of David as a forerunner of the Messiah. The legends about him were so enduring that seven or eight hundred years after his death the Christians of Europe sometimes wove those tales into biblical stories and portrayed Alexander as a saint in search of paradise.

2

Mithridates

I tell the tale that I heard told.
Mithridates, he died old.

Those last lines of a poem by A. E. Housman refer to a king of ancient times who worked out a unique method of protecting himself against being poisoned by some scheming enemy. When he was still quite young he learned that if a person swallowed a small amount of poison each day over a long span of time he could develop an immunity to it. And so that was what he did. Day after day, month ofter month, year after year, Mithridates took his daily dose of poison. Then he ate and drank fearlessly any food or drink that was offered to him. As a result, he did indeed live to be seventy-one years old, and he did not die of poison.

His Country, Pontus

Mithridates was born about 134 B.C., the eldest son of the king of Pontus. Pontus was one of the ancient countries in what is now Turkey—a wild and beautiful land on the edge of the Black Sea, eastward of Lydia and Phrygia, two other Asia Minor countries that figure in many tales of the ancient world. (Among them, for instance, are the stories of *Croesus* and *Midas* in this book.)

His father's name was Mithridates also, and his younger brothers had the same name as well. This custom in Pontus of naming *all* of a king's sons Mithridates was made a little less confusing by giving each Mithridates a second name, which was what people generally called him. This Mithridates' second name was Eupator, which meant the Good Father.

At the time of Mithridates Eupator's birth, Rome had become the mighty power of the Mediterranean world. Her legions were in territories, westward and northward, that had been practically unknown to Alexander—Spain and Gaul. Her legions were in Greece also, and in northern Africa. And in Asia Minor the country of Pontus was ringed around by countries held by the Romans.

Mithridates Eupator's father was a bold king with hopes of challenging Roman might and keeping Pontus for himself. Mithridates Eupator's mother, Queen Laodice, was against such a course. She had only one desire. She wanted to live richly and comfortably with none of the fear and uncertainty that would come of defying the Romans. As a result, when her husband, young Mithridates Eupator's father, was assassinated, many people in Pontus believed she had arranged for his murder.

Since Mithridates Eupator was only twelve, Laodice was appointed to rule as queen regent until the boy was of age. She quickly made peace with Rome, agreed that Pontus should be a sort of dependency of the Roman Empire, and settled down to enjoy a rich and easy life.

Mithridates' Escape

Mithridates Eupator was an intelligent boy. He pondered on what had happened to his father. He pondered on something that had been happening in a neighboring kingdom also. There another queen regent was ruling. That queen had five sons and one after another the sons met unexpected deaths as they approached the age when they would be old enough to take over the country's rule.

Mithridates decided that he did not want to meet with an unexpected death. It was at this time that he found out how to make himself immune to poison and began to swallow a little every day.

But he also realized that there were other dangers to his life than poison. He loved to hunt, and he thought about how many accidents could be arranged to kill a hunter.

One day when he was fourteen, he went out on a hunt with a group of friends whom he trusted completely. He and the friends did not return. Days passed and then months, and still Mithridates and his companions were absent. The queen regent puzzled over the matter for a while. Then she decided that her son had met with a real accident and stopped thinking about him.

Meanwhile, Mithridates and his friends were living a gypsy life in the wild

forests and mountains of Pontus. Sometimes they stopped at a secluded castle of some noble whom Mithridates knew was loyal. He and his friends replaced their worn-out clothing or horses. But they never stayed long. And no matter where he was Mithridates took his daily poison and ate only the meat of animals he shot himself.

For seven years he lived this wild, free life. He grew tall and strong and handsome and became a wonderful horseman.

Then, when he was twenty-one, he left the forests and rode into the rich city of Sinope, the capital of Pontus. The citizens were dazzled by his beauty and assurance. Unlike most of them, who copied Greek ways and wore Greek clothes, Mithridates wore Persian trousers with a jeweled sword thrust into his belt. This only made him seem more wonderful to the populace. Then, hearing that he was Mithridates Eupator, their true king, the people crowded about him to follow him as he rode to the palace where the queen mother was living.

Mithridates had his mother seized and kept under custody in private quarters but she was not harmed in any way.

The Mithridatic Wars

For the first few years after Mithridates claimed his throne he devoted himself to enriching and beautifying his country and to strengthening the army and the fleet.

Then he began a career of conquest throughout the neighboring kingdoms. This was a direct challenge to Rome, which considered itself in authority in these territories. Mithridates was undaunted by the Roman power that mobilized against him and his army. He sent some of his forces to Greece to distract Roman troops in that area and in one victorious battle after another swept his troops from kingdom to kingdom until he had won the whole of Asia Minor. Then, as ruthless as most conquerors of his time, he ordered the massacre of all Romans living in Asia Minor.

After this, Rome redoubled its efforts against him and finally, in 84 B.C., Mithridates' armies both in Asia Minor and in Greece were defeated. Mithridates was left with no country in his possession but Pontus. History calls this the First Mithridatic War.

But Mithridates was a determined king. Within a year he was again challenging Roman might in Asia Minor. This time he was more successful. The Romans were worsted and made peace with Mithridates to end what is called the second Mithridatic War.

But Rome was determined also. Within a few years the struggle was renewed. The Roman general Lucullus marched against Mithridates and his troops and managed to destroy his army. Mithridates had to flee into Armenia. Still this stubborn king had enough power and appeal to gather yet another army around him. But now Pompey, a Roman general who rivaled the great Caesar, became supreme commander of the Roman legions and he forced Mithridates back, back, back into the last of the provinces remaining to him. Finally, in 63 B. C., Mithridates' own troops, led by his son, mutinied against him. Mithridates, giving up at last, had a slave kill him. That was the end of the Third Mithridatic War.

By his wit, his intelligence, and his strength, Mithridates had managed to avoid the many dooms planned for him and to become the greatest threat to Rome since the days of Hannibal of Carthage. In the end, though, Rome was too powerful for him.

3
Harold Fairhair

It was not because Harold of Norway's hair was so especially fair that men gave him his nickname but because it was so long and tangled. And the reason it had grown so long was because Harold had sworn a great vow. He would not cut his hair or comb it until he was king of all Norway.

The Norway of Harold's Time

Harold lived in the middle of the ninth century (more than a thousand years after Alexander's time). He was the son of Black Halfdans, who called himself king of Norway, but the area over which Halfdans ruled was very small. In those years, that wild, cold country was still divided among hundreds of landowning chieftains. The chieftains ruled the people who lived on their domains however they wished and spent most of their time going a-viking. This meant sailing off in their swift, beautiful longships to lands in every direction, to trade and to raid—mostly raid. They brought back rich booty from these voyages but it hardly benefited anyone that they did so. For the vikings, as these seafaring Norsemen were called, were pirates who fought each other, as well as the people of other countries, on land and at sea, every man for himself.

Then, after Black Halfdans' death, Harold became king, and an old Norse saga tells of what happened next. He fell in love.

Harold's Vow

The maiden who won Harold's heart was named Gyda. She was the daughter of the king of Hordaland, an area that is now part of Norway. "Marvelous it seems to me," Gyda remarked to Harold, "that there is no king who will make Norway his own and be sole ruler thereof, as King Gorm has done in Denmark and Eric in Uppsala."

Harold thought about Gyda's words, and the more he thought about them the truer they seemed. At last he made his vow. "I will not cut nor comb my hair until all Norway is mine."

Harold's Conquests

He readied his longships and manned them, and as the weeks passed his hair grew longer and more tangled. At last the ships were ready, and he sailed off to attack some vikings who were preying on ships off the west coast of Norway. He fought with these vikings and defeated them and made them acknowledge that he was their king. But that was only one group of Norsemen.

He planned a new attack on some vikings farther to the south and sailed off to fight them. He stood at the dragon's head prow of his ship, and his long hair streamed out in the wind beneath his helmet. It was then that men began calling him Harold Fairhair.

Harold Fairhair triumphed in that battle. And now chieftains everywhere in Norway began to realize that he was determined to conquer them all. They began rallying their men and fitting out their longships to sail against Harold Fairhair and strike him down. But Harold moved more rapidly than they did and sailed to meet them. He surprised them in the waters of a deep, wide fjord called Hafrsfjord, and the battle was on.

The fight was so long and hard that for years afterward men told of the battle of Hafrsfjord and recited the names of the men who had died during the course of it. But at its end Harold Fairhair was the victor.

Many of the chieftains who had been defeated by Harold still refused to admit that he was their king, to submit to any laws he wanted to make, or to pay what taxes he imposed. But they had to sail away from Norway to save their lives and to find new homes on the islands of the Hebrides or in Iceland. All who remained in Norway had to bow their heads and acknowledge Harold as their king.

Harold spent two more years making sure that no one would dispute his authority. At last he decided that he had fulfilled his vow. He cut his long, matted, tangled hair.

And then, according to the saga, he married Gyda, the maiden who had inspired his great achievement.

The Consequences of Harold's Battles

Harold's victories over the vikings did more than unite the people of Norway under one ruler. Iceland was settled chiefly by Norsemen who had fled from his power. Eric the Red, the son of one of those Norse exiles in Iceland, discovered the great island of Greenland and established a settlement there. And it was Eric's son, Leif the Lucky, who voyaged from Greenland west-over-seas to discover America and establish a colony there almost five hundred years before Christopher Columbus made his voyage to the New World.

4
William the Conqueror

TEN SIXTY-SIX is a date that almost everyone remembers—the date of the Norman Conquest of England.

William, Duke of Normandy, who led the successful Norman invasion of the island across the channel from France, is the great central figure of the events of 1066. But two kings of England play important parts in the story as well. And a surprise Norse attack on England, plus some freakish weather over the English channel, also had something to do with William's success.

William's Birth and Childhood

William was born in A.D. 1027 in the country of Normandy on the northern coast of France. This was an area that had first been raided by Norsemen and then ceded to them more than a hundred years before William was born, and it was called Normandy for that reason.

Duke Robert, who was known as the Magnificent, was William's father. And although the boy was an illegitimate child he was acknowledged as his father's heir when he was still very young. In 1035, his father died, and William became the Duke of Normandy at the age of eight.

For a few years his guardians handled the affairs of the dukedom but William was a spirited boy. He quickly began to do well in all the knightly skills of riding, hunting, and falconry, and when he was still quite young he was able to assert himself as a leader. After this, when the men who were called his guardians rode out to put down the various rebellions that troubled the dukedom, William rode with them, learning how to be a soldier.

William's Cousin and His Promise

The first seeds of William's ambition to be king of England were planted during the years when he was growing up. In exile in Normandy during this period was Edward, son of Ethelred the Unready of England, who had been driven from his country by the Danish conqueror Canute. Edward was much older than William and devoted to the religious life as the active boy was not. But Edward, who was not unhappy in exile because he admired everything French, also admired the bold, brave young Duke of Normandy. Most fatefully of all, he and William were cousins, related through Edward's mother.

The exiled Edward told his young cousin that he, William, had the best claim to the English crown after his own, once the Danes were driven out. William took this statement very seriously.

In 1041, when William was fourteen, Edward was recalled to England to take over the rule of the country from the Danish king, Hardicanute. Edward became a good and kindly king, so pious that his people called him the Confessor. After he had been king for some time, William visited him. William found his cousin still friendly to him, and before he left William made sure that Edward repeated his words about William's right to the English throne. In fact, he won from Edward the promise that he would name William as his successor.

William's Marriage

While Edward the Confessor reigned in England, William increased his power in Normandy. Grown to manhood, he showed himself a brilliant soldier. There were no more rebellions in his dukedom. Finally he challenged his onetime ally, the King of France, who was not nearly so powerful in those years as the duke of a great area like Normandy. From the King of France William won another large province, Maine, as a part of his dukedom.

Meantime, he felt that he was strengthening his claim to the English crown when he married the Princess Mathilda of Flanders in 1053. She was a direct descendant of Alfred the Great.

Harold of England

In England, very few of the Saxon nobles paid much heed to the fact that across the channel there was a French duke who believed he would be England's next king. Most heedless of all were Earl Godwin and his sons. Earl Godwin was one of the most powerful nobles in the land. He had supported the Danish king Canute in 1013 and had risen to become Earl of Wessex. Later, when Canute's sons had shown themselves much less able to govern England than their father, Earl Godwin had helped to bring Edward the Confessor back from exile. The importance of the Godwins increased when Edward married one of Earl Godwin's daughters. The Earl's oldest son, Harold, became Earl of East Anglia, and another son, Tostig, became one of Edward's favorites.

The Godwins had their ups and downs. For a while they were out of favor and exiled themselves in Ireland. Then in 1061, they returned to England and soon became more important than ever. The old earl died and his oldest son, Harold, who was heir to all his great estates, became the most powerful man in England next to the king. Harold had always been a leader of men. Now he further proved his abilities with an expedition against the Welsh in the west of England.

There began to be talk that Harold Godwinson might be the next king of England. The talk spread. Soon nobles and commoners alike began to think of Harold as Edward's logical successor.

Harold's Meeting with William

In 1063, Harold, Tostig, and a younger brother went on a pilgrimage to Rome. On their return, their ship was wrecked off the coast of France. They landed safely but were seized by a local nobleman. The nobleman was a vassal of William, Duke of Normandy, and when William heard the identities of the Englishmen the nobleman was holding, he demanded that Harold and his brothers be turned over to him.

Harold and William had heard about each other all their lives. When they met for the first time they found they had much in common. William was tall and dark, Harold, sturdy and blond, but both were born leaders, skilled in knightly games. For a while they enjoyed themselves with tourneys and balls.

But William's ambition to be king of England was stronger than any friendship he felt for Harold. Soon Harold and his brothers found themselves under a sort of arrest. They could continue to enjoy themselves at court but they could not leave and were watched constantly.

News came to Harold of revolts and uprisings in different parts of England. He was anxious to get home and help to restore order. He asked William to set him and his brothers free. William said he would do so only if Harold promised that he would not accept the English crown himself but would support William's claim. At last, desperate to return to England, Harold swore an oath that he would do as William wished. William kept the youngest Godwin as a hostage and let Harold and Tostig go back to England.

Harold Named King

As soon as Harold was in England he renounced the oath he had made to William. These were times when oaths were not broken lightly and Harold was an honorable man. But he insisted that he had taken the oath under duress, which meant that it was not binding. Most of his countrymen agreed with him, but his brother, Tostig, did not. Tostig was anxious about the fate of the young brother left behind in Normandy. He and Harold quarreled. When the people of Northumbria, Tostig's earldom, revolted against him, Harold did not support his brother. Driven from his lands, Tostig took refuge in Norway with King Harold Hardrada.

Meantime, Edward the Confessor had become old and ill. He was concerned with the fate of England after his death. And finally he decided that Harold, one of the most popular men in England, would be the most able king to succeed him. Just before he died, early in 1066, he named Harold Godwinson as his successor.

After Edward's death and burial, the council, or witan, of England agreed with Edward's choice and named Harold the next king. Harold was crowned and assumed the throne.

William's Answer

When William heard that Edward was dead and Harold crowned king of England he was outraged, feeling that he had been betrayed by both men.

Edward had promised him the crown, and Harold had sworn an oath to support him.

William began at once to gather his army and prepare for an invasion of England, to take by force what he felt was his by promise, oath, and inheritance.

Harold Prepares

Harold soon had news in his turn of William's plans to invade England and he began his own preparations to resist the invasion.

Harold had a far different sort of army than William. The French fighting men were chiefly knights who devoted their lives to war and the hunt. England's soldiers were not full-time fighting men but farmers who left their fields to take up arms only when they were summoned by their king or over-lord. Still they were good soldiers and came quickly to Harold's call. Harold also fitted out a fleet to ride at anchor off the southern coast, prepared to fight William's fleet when it came across the channel.

Then, with everything ready, Harold and his men began their wait for William and the Normans. The warm days of summer arrived, and the Saxons, waiting vainly for the invasion, began to worry about their crops.

Meanwhile, William's forces on the other side of the channel were having worries of their own. When the fleet and army were at last ready to sail the winds over the channel suddenly began blowing to the east so that they could not sail across the channel westward. William and his men were land-bound.

For a week, then two weeks, contrary winds prevailed. Some of William's men began to say that the wind was a sign from heaven that their venture was ill-omened. But William refused to give up his plans to win England. So William waited on his side of the channel. And Harold waited on his.

The Norsemen Intervene

Suddenly, Harold received word that a large force of Norsemen, led by Harold Hardrada (or Hardcounsel) of Norway, had landed on the far north-ern coast of England. They were raiding and terrorizing the people there. Harold's brother, Tostig, was with Harold Hardrada. Duke William, who was friendly with the Norse Harold, had undoubtedly encouraged him to attack England at this time.

Harold of England had no choice. He had to end his watch for William in the south and hurry north to fight the Norsemen. He and his men managed to surprise the invaders at Stamford Bridge. There was a fearful battle, and in the end Harold and his Saxons won the day. Harold Hardrada was killed. So were many of his men and Tostig also lost his life in the battle.

Harold's tired and wounded Saxons had no time to rejoice in their victory. Word came from the south. The wind across the channel had shifted. William and his Norman host had crossed over from France and landed in England.

Once again, Harold had no choice, but now it was an exhausted army that he had to hurry by forced marches to meet William, the invader from Normandy.

The Battle of Hastings, October 14, 1066

Harold brought his men to the south sooner than anyone had thought possible. He found that William had been setting fire to villages and pillaging the land to hasten Harold's coming. Still Harold sent word to the French duke that he would give him all the gold and silver he desired if he would forget the forced oath of two years before and return to his own land without warfare. William sent back the reply that Harold was a usurper and a perjurer. He refused any offers of peace. Both sides then prepared for battle.

English history and legend are full of accounts of this battle. The Saxons, under Harold, formed a shield wall on the heights above Hastings. The Norman knights on their horses rushed the shield wall with their lances poised and were rebuffed time and again.

One story tells that the Norman knights at last feigned retreat back across the valley and lured the Saxons after them. There the Saxon ranks and shield wall were broken, and the Normans turned and had a better chance against them. Other stories deny that the retreat was a ruse and say that the Saxons really were triumphing over the Normans, and that William rallied his fleeing men and forced them to turn again and attack.

However it happened, Harold stood on the heights above Hastings, urging his men to hold their ground. As he stood there by his standard a stray arrow struck him in the eye. He fell, mortally wounded.

With Harold's fall, the Saxons, already tired and confused, went to pieces. The fighting continued into the darkness. But there was no doubt about the outcome of the battle. William, Duke of Normandy, was the victor. England was his.

William as a Conqueror

After the defeat of Harold at the Battle of Hastings, William marched on to London, the chief city of England, and was crowned king of England on Christmas day, 1066.

All resistance to him did not end with Harold's defeat and death. The earls in the northern provinces rose against William time and again during the next few years. Finally William sent a host of soldiers to lay waste to all the northern counties that still resisted him. Thousands were killed. Miles of land were burned over. This was the punishment that came to be called "the harrying of the north." At last all of England resigned itself to the rule of William the Conqueror.

The Changes He Brought

William of Normandy brought a new way of life to England. He took over all the land of the great Saxon nobles and divided it among his own men. Castles and private fortresses in the French style were built instead of the farmhouses and manors that the Saxons had known. Life was organized along feudal lines. Knighthood and chivalry and the manners later described in Malory's *Morte d'Arthur* came to England in these days.

The French language became the language of the court and all the nobility. Only farmers and tradesmen still spoke Saxon. As a result changes came to the English language that endure to this day. The Saxon farmers who tended livestock called their creatures by their names in Saxon—oxen, cows, calves, sheep, pigs. But when the creatures were killed, and their meat was dressed and cooked and served to the Normans, the meat of the ox was called by the creature's French name, *boeuf,* or beef. Calf meat was *veau,* or veal. Sheep was *mouton,* or mutton. Pig was *Porc.*

The famous novel *Ivanhoe* by Sir Walter Scott gives a fictionalized version of this period in England's history, dramatizing the plight of the conquered Saxons and their hopes of restoring the crown to some heir of Edward the Confessor.

Still, the Norman Conquest was not without advantages for England. The country grew stronger as William forced everyone to give allegiance to him. He had the whole country surveyed, acre by acre, and the numbers of people and even of livestock recorded in a famous volume called the Domesday, or Doomsday Book. (Curiously, the word *doom* is Anglo-Saxon for law and that word was used instead of the French word *loi*.)

Under William's rule, England was allied with William's other country, Normandy, so that they became one kingdom. Now every advance in civilization that was made in Europe was soon felt in England as well. England was no longer a far northern outpost cut off from Europe by the channel.

William the Conqueror was in France when he died in 1087, and it was in France that he was buried, but his mark remained on the land that he had conquered. Two of his sons followed him as kings of England. First there was William II, known as William Rufus, then Henry I, known as Beauclerc. Stephen, a grandson of the Conqueror, followed them. His reign was troubled and chaotic, and after him there came a grandson of Henry I, the son of his daughter Matilda who had married a French nobleman, Geoffrey Plantagenet, Count of Anjou. This grandson of the first Henry, Henry II, was the first of a long line of Plantagenet kings who included the famous Richard the Lionhearted.

So the French ties and the French influence in England lingered on for more than two hundred years after the conquest by William, Duke of Normandy.

5
Richard the Lionhearted

RICHARD THE LIONHEARTED, or coeur de Lion, as he was called in France, won his fame as a crusader. In his efforts to help the Christians of Europe recapture Jerusalem from the Moslems, he showed all the knightly virtues of valor, daring, and gallantry that were most admired in his time. Even his bad luck had such a romantic flavor to it that although he was not often in England during the years that he was king, he was a hero to his countrymen and became an English symbol of chivalry.

Richard's Birth and Childhood

Richard was born in 1157, almost a hundred years after the Norman Conquest had brought French ideals and ways of life to England. He was the third son of King Henry II and his wife, Eleanor of Aquitaine. Soon there were two younger brothers, Geoffrey and John.

The years of his childhood were full of turmoil and family difficulties that hardly seemed likely to shape a gallant and courteous knight. His mother and father quarreled so bitterly that when Richard was thirteen his mother left his father and set up her own court in France. Soon she had encouraged her sons to rebel against their father. Richard was just sixteen when he joined his brothers in this revolt. Little was accomplished by this battling except that Richard's brothers grew jealous of his intelligence, courage, and ability and soon began plotting against him. Before long Richard was battling against his brothers. In the course of this warfare his oldest brother, Henry, died. Then John, the youngest brother, who had always been the father's favorite, finally managed to provoke a quarrel between Richard and their father.

In this new difficulty Richard found a friend and ally in King Philip Augustus of France. It was 1189 when Richard, with Philip's support, again went to war against his father. This time Henry II was defeated. Philip of France won several valuable territories as a reward for his aid; Richard won the right to succeed his father. King Henry was already dying. Two days after peace was made Henry was dead, and Richard, aged thirty-two, was crowned King of England.

The Third Crusade

After all his efforts to win the crown, Richard showed little interest in ruling once he was king. He had another great ambition. He wanted to help launch and lead a new crusade to the Holy Land, and he was glad to be king because of the power it gave him to do so.

There were urgent reasons for a new crusade. Almost a hundred years before, the First Crusade had taken thousands of men from all over Europe to Asia Minor. The goal then had been to drive away the Moslems who ruled Jerusalem and make it possible again for the Christians of Europe to visit the holy shrines in the ancient city. The First Crusade had been successful. Jerusalem and many other cities around it had been captured. A Latin Kingdom of Jerusalem had been established, and various European princes had been named governors or kings of the different parts of the new kingdom.

But all had not gone smoothly with this new Latin Kingdom in the Holy Land. The European princes had quarreled among themselves. There were intrigues and plots. Then, about fifty years after the First Crusade, one of the cities near Jerusalem was taken by the Moslems. A Second Crusade was organized and sent out from Europe to recapture the city. That crusade had been a failure.

Now, in 1189, as Richard became king of England, a far greater disaster than the loss of one city had overtaken the Latin Kingdom of Jerusalem. A brilliant Moslem warrior and leader named Saladin had been sweeping his armies across the Middle East. He had taken control of Egypt and extended his rule over most of Syria. Finally, he captured most of the cities held by the European Christians, including Jerusalem itself.

A call from the Pope went out across Christendom, urging a new crusade. Richard had been dreaming of being the leader of such a project even as he fought his final battles with his father. Philip Augustus of France was also committed to a new crusade.

As soon as Richard became king, he did everything he could to raise money. He imposed new taxes, sold titles and honors, and forced his subjects to contribute to a crusade in dozens of ways. He began gathering an army and readying a fleet. There was a rift in his friendship with Philip Augustus at this time, but Philip was also busy raising men, money, and supplies. In 1190, both kings took their vows as crusaders, and first Philip then Richard set forth for the Holy Land with their armies.

The Journey to Jerusalem

Richard had a transport fleet of one hundred ships carrying four thousand men at arms and an equal number of foot soldiers. The fleet sailed as far as the island of Sicily and then put in at a harbor. The men disembarked to set up winter quarters. Philip Augustus and his forces were already settled on the island when Richard and his men arrived. The strained relations between the two kings were not improved through the winter months. By springtime, when they were able to resume their journey, they no longer even pretended to be friends.

Still Richard did not go directly to the Holy Land. Instead, he sailed his forces to the island of Cyprus, which was a possession of the Byzantine Empire. Disembarking there, he set about conquering the island. It was not a wasted effort for the island later became a useful outpost for crusaders, and they left many evidences of their presence there. Tourists visit Cyprus today to see ruins that remain from the days of Richard the Lionhearted.

Richard also found romance on Cyprus. The princess Berengaria, daughter of Sancho VI of Navarre, was visiting the island, and she and Richard fell in love. Richard was already betrothed, and had been for some time, to Philip Augustus' sister, Alais. He canceled that engagement and was soon married to Berengaria.

The wives of soldiers often accompanied their husbands to the wars in those days, so Berengaria sailed on to the Holy Land with Richard. She did not stay there long, however, but returned to her home to await the outcome of Richard's battles. As things turned out, it was a long time before she saw him again.

Richard in the Holy Land

Richard and Philip arrived in the Holy Land with their forces in 1191 and landed outside the city of Acre, which is now part of Israel. The European princes of the Latin Kingdom of Jerusalem, and other crusaders who had arrived earlier, had been besieging Acre for two years. Jealousy and quarreling among the leaders had kept them from making much progress with the siege. Richard's arrival changed everything. He was full of energy and was tactful and courteous as well. Somehow he soothed everyone's ruffled feelings and inspired all the crusaders with new enthusiasm. Before long Acre had surrendered.

Philip left for home at this point but Richard moved the army's base to another city, fortified it, and then turned his efforts to besieging Saladin who had established his headquarters in Jerusalem.

Saladin and Richard

Richard, the brave champion of Christendom who was now known as the Lionhearted, at last met his match as he faced Saladin, the leader of the Moslems, or Saracens, as the crusaders called all Mohammedans. Saladin was more than a shrewd soldier. He was also a cultivated, intelligent, and generous man.

As Richard pressed the siege on Jerusalem and Saladin resisted, messengers went back and forth between the two men, with offered terms and refusals. Gradually, the two men grew to respect each other, and, in spite of the state of war between them, various courtesies were exchanged. Later, many legends would be told about Richard and Saladin. One story related that on an extremely hot day Saladin sent a messenger to Richard's tent outside the city walls to present the English king with a dish of sherbet from Saladin's own table. The sherbet was a rare delicacy, cooled by snow brought from the mountains.

After the siege had gone on for some months, both Richard and Saladin had to recognize a stalemate. Saladin offered generous truce terms. He promised that cities the crusaders had captured might remain theirs, and that they would also be allowed to retain a narrow strip of coast line. Saladin would continue to hold Jerusalem, but he promised the Christians that they would

be allowed free access to their holy shrines within the city.

Richard agreed to the terms. In October of 1192 he boarded a ship and set sail for England.

His Shipwreck

Richard's misfortunes began when his ship was wrecked in the Adriatic Sea. He and some companions reached shore safely, and then Richard decided to travel overland across Europe toward England. However, he remembered the bad feeling that had arisen between German and Austrian crusaders and the English. He decided that it might be safer for him to travel in disguise across Austria and Germany in case some prince might see an opportunity for revenge.

But even though he was disguised and using a different name he was recognized. He was near Vienna when he was kidnapped on the orders of Leopold II, Margrave of Austria. Then he was taken to the castle of Dürnstein and held prisoner by Leopold. Leopold told Richard that he intended to hold him for a high ransom and that until his terms were met no one would be allowed to know where the English king was being held.

John's Activities in England

Richard's plight was even worse than he knew for he was not aware of the way his youngest brother, John, had been behaving ever since his departure from England in 1190. John, who had been given many lands and titles by Richard after he became king, was repaying his brother's generosity with treachery. First John led a rebellion against the administrator Richard had appointed to manage the kingdom while he was gone. Then John had himself acknowledged temporary ruler of England and heir to the crown. After this, he began to abuse his power by ruling harshly and imposing heavy taxes.

When news came to John from Leopold II that Richard was being held prisoner somewhere in Austria, John was happy to hear it. He began conspiring with Richard's onetime friend, Philip of France, for ways in which they might prolong Richard's imprisonment and how they might divide England between them.

So the months passed and Richard remained a prisoner in the Austrian castle. He had no word from the outside world and no idea of when, if ever, he would be released.

Blondel, the Minstrel

According to legend, Richard's favorite minstrel, or court singer, who was named Blondel, had accompanied the king to the Holy Land and was with him as he began his journey home. But when Richard was kidnaped, Blondel had no clue as to where he had been taken. Blondel was devoted to his king and began at once to try to find him.

It was the custom then for many minstrels to travel about the country going from one castle or manor house to another. They brought both news and entertainment and were welcomed and well rewarded everywhere. So Blondel went from castle to castle. Once he was inside the castle walls, and after he had entertained his hosts and their guests, Blondel would wander about the castle yard, looking for any windows that seemed to give on dungeon cells. When he found any that seemed likely he would softly sing the first verse of a song that only he and Richard knew. Then he would listen, hoping for a response.

At castle after castle he heard nothing. Then he came to the castle at Dürnstein. He began to sing under a barred window in the courtyard. But he had not finished the verse before a voice he knew floated down from the barred window, singing the words with him and then going on to the next verse. Blondel, the minstrel, had found his king.

Richard's Release

However Richard's whereabouts were actually discovered, and in spite of all John's and Phillip's plans to keep him imprisoned, Richard's captivity finally came to an end. Some complicated European politics caused the Austrian emperor to demand that Leopold surrender Richard to him. Then the Emperor used Richard as a bargaining weapon for something he wanted. When he obtained that, he asked Richard to swear fealty to him and then demanded a huge ransom for his release. Richard's subjects in England collected the sum required. At last Richard was set free and returned home.

In England he learned about some of John's treachery, but, still a generous brother, he forgave him and then set about repairing the damage John had done in his absence.

Philip of France was not so easy to forgive and soon Richard was in France fighting him.

Saucy Castle

Richard's previous treaties with Philip of France forbade him to build fortresses in Philip's domains. In defiance of this prohibition, Richard was soon building a splendid fortified castle on a crag above the Seine River near Les Andelys, France, to defend Normandy. He flaunted his defiance further by calling this beautiful castle Château Gaillard, or Saucy Castle. The ruins of Château Gaillard still stand in France.

Richard's Death

In 1199, when Richard was forty-two years old, he was fighting a minor battle in France with a rather unimportant enemy, the Viscount of Limoges. During the course of the battle he was hit in the shoulder by a crossbow bolt. He died of the wound several days later.

All through his youth he had fought with his father, King Henry II. But in spite of those quarrels, Richard had loved his parent. By his own desire he was buried at his father's feet in the church of Fontevrault.

He was a loyal brother also. In spite of the way his brother John had betrayed him during his absence, he had arranged that John should succeed him on the throne of England.

John as King

John had no changes of heart after becoming king of England in 1199. He continued his self-seeking course of misrule until the Pope in Rome felt forced to interfere. The Pope's way of punishing John was to deny everyone in England the sacraments of the church so long as John was king. John promised to reform and won back control of his kingdom. Then he began at once to plan a war on Philip of France, with whom he had once conspired against Richard.

By this time, however, all the noblemen of England were enraged by their ruler. And it was from King John, the brother of the gallant Richard, that the English barons finally won the Magna Carta, the first great English bill of rights. King John signed it at Runnymede in 1215. A year later, John died, still struggling to triumph over the barons, the French, and everyone else who thwarted him.

The Plantagenets

Richard and John were both Plantagenet kings, which meant that they were descendants of Geoffrey, Count of Anjou, of France. The word "plantagenet" means broom plant. The broom plant grew in great profusion in Anjou and turned the open countryside into a golden blaze in early summer. Because Geoffrey liked to wear a sprig of the plant in his cap he became known as "Plantagenet." The last of the Plantagenets to rule England was Richard III.

Richard in Literature

Richard and his crusaders play important roles in Sir Walter Scott's novel *Ivanhoe*. He and his brother John also figure in *The Merry Adventures of Robin Hood*.

PART TWO

GOOD AND BELOVED KINGS

Ay, every inch a king. . . .
  King Lear, WILLIAM SHAKESPEARE (1564–1616)

David of Israel

King Arthur and His Round Table

Charlemagne

Alfred the Great

King Canute

Henry of Navarre

6

David of Israel

David was a shepherd king, a harpist, and a singer of sweet songs. He was also
a warrior king who defeated the Philistines and united the twelve tribes of
Israel into one strong nation. Fearless and bold, sensitive and poetic, David is
a king equally beloved by Jews, Christians, and Moslems.

His Country and His Times

David was born about 1,000 B.C. (No one can be exactly sure of any date
that long ago.) The Hebrew tribes had long since undergone their years of
bondage in Egypt and made their way back to their homeland in Asia Minor.
But in spite of the sufferings they had known together and the religion they
shared the tribes were not united. Ten tribes had settled in the northern part
of the country and that area was known as Israel. Two tribes were in a
southern area called Judah. For a long time none of the tribes had any especially chosen ruler but relied on local wise men, judges, or prophets for
leadership, and the northern and southern tribes were often in conflict.

Then, in the south, in Judah, an especially bold and warlike judge named
Saul won for himself the name and authority of king. He would have liked to
unite all the tribes under his rule, but he had little time for such a project.
Year after year, most of Saul's energies had to be spent in fighting Judah's
chief enemies, the Philistines.

The Philistines lived along the coast of Asia Minor west of Judah, and they
also controlled a strip of land between Judah and Israel where they had a
fortified town called Jerusalem. Many scholars believe these Philistines were
descendants of the Cretans who had emigrated from their island about 1,200
B.C. (See the story of King Minos.) Certainly the Philistines were a rich,
highly civilized people who had built fine trading cities along the coast and

followed many Greek ways. They were also a people who seemed bent on the conquest of the Hebrew tribes who lived in the hills to the east of them. Year after year they sent their armies out against them. And though King Saul managed to keep them from being wholly victorious, he could not finally defeat them. That accomplishment fell to David.

David, the Shepherd Boy

The Bible relates David's story. He was the youngest son of a pious farmer of Judah named Jesse. A handsome boy, "ruddy, and withal of a beautiful countenance and goodly to look on," David was still the least regarded of his father's sons and was sent out into the fields to tend the sheep. David whiled away the lonely hours by playing a handmade harp and singing songs of his own invention.

His talent for music-making was what brought him first to the attention of King Saul. Saul, as he grew older, was prone to black moods of depression and anger. One day, one of his men told him that David, the son of Jesse, was a wonderfully sweet singer and that his music might soothe the king. Saul sent for David. David came, played for the king, and pleased him so well that Saul asked him to stay on in his court to play for him whenever he was sad.

David and Goliath

One of the best known stories about David is the account of how he killed the giant Goliath. This is probably only a legend for the Bible itself gives two different versions of the slaying of the giant. One version simply tells that Goliath was killed by a Hebrew soldier. The other story, as told in the First Book of Samuel, is much more dramatic.

The Philistines were again besieging the Hebrews. They were encamped on a hill facing Saul's army which was encamped on another hill across a valley. Every day, a giant of a man, covered from head to foot in brass armor, walked down the hill from the Philistines' camp to shout a challenge to the Hebrews. He cried out that his name was Goliath, that he came from the city of Gath, and that he was willing to fight in single combat any man that the Hebrews chose to send against him.

"If he be able to fight with me and to kill me," shouted Goliath, "then will we be your servants; but if I prevail against him, and kill him, then shall ye be our servants and serve us."

The challenge made the Hebrews tremble. Not a man in Saul's army dared face the giant. It began to seem that the Philistines would triumph without the need for any battle at all and that Saul's men would finally disband and go home defeated by their fear of the giant.

Then David came to Saul's camp, bringing some gifts of food for his brothers who were serving in Saul's army. David heard Goliath's challenge. And suddenly David the shepherd was crying out that he would fight the giant.

David's brothers only laughed at him, but the other soldiers were less scornful and hurried to Saul to tell him that the Hebrews had a champion at last. Then Saul sent for David and told the boy that he was too young and slight to fight a giant.

David told Saul of some of his exploits as a shepherd. He said that he had once killed four lions and three bears with his naked hands after the beasts had attacked his flock. At last Saul agreed to let David face Goliath. He offered him armor to wear, but David refused it. David insisted that he would go as he was, dressed in his shepherd's tunic. For a weapon, he would use his sling-shot. He went to a nearby brook and chose five smooth stones to shoot from it. Then he walked down the hill and out into the valley and called out to the Philistine camp that he was accepting Goliath's challenge.

The giant came striding down the hill, saw the boy, and laughed. But David still spoke boldly. He said that he faced Goliath and all the Philistines in the name of the lord of Israel, who would protect him and deliver the giant into his hands. Then he took one of the stones from his shepherd's bag, fitted it into his slingshot and let it fly.

The stone struck Goliath on the forehead, and the giant pitched forward onto the ground. David ran forward, seized the giant's sword, and cut off his head.

For a moment the Philistines stood still, unable to believe that their champion was really killed. Then they turned to flee. The Hebrews, shouting their triumph, raced after them, pursuing them over hills and valleys all the way back to Philistia.

David was the hero of all the Hebrews. He rode at the king's side as Saul went back into his chief city of Gibeah. The townspeople cheered him and sang his praises. "Saul has slain his thousands," they cried, "and David his tens of thousands." Saul showed his gratitude by making David a captain in the army and by giving him one of his daughters as a wife. But Saul was also jealous of David's triumph, and his jealousy grew as everyone kept praising the young man.

David and Jonathan

Jonathan was Saul's son, the heir to the throne. It might have seemed logical for him to be jealous of David also. Instead, he and David became friends at their first meeting. They were such good, loyal friends that the phrase "David and Jonathan" is a synonym for friendship to this day.

It was fortunate for David that Jonathan was his friend, for Saul's jealousy at last caused the king to wish David killed. Saul sent David on a mission against the Philistines, hoping that he would not survive, but David accomplished the mission and returned safely. Next Saul arranged to have David killed while he slept in his bed. But Saul's daughter, Michal, who had become David's wife, heard of the plot. She warned David to flee and put an image in his bed in his place. After that Jonathan was sure that his father would make a third attempt on David's life, and so he told David to hide outside the city until he could learn his father's plans. They arranged for the signal Jonathan would use to let David know if it was safe to return or not.

David hid, as Jonathan had suggested. Two days later, he saw Jonathan and a young boy walk out into a nearby field. Then Jonathan stopped and shot several arrows into the air. "Go fetch them," he told the boy. And then, as the boy ran after them, David heard Jonathan call, "Is not the arrow beyond thee? Make speed, haste, stay not." It was the signal to David that he must leave Gibeah to avoid death.

The boy picked up the arrows, took them back to Jonathan, and then Jonathan sent him away. David came forth from his hiding place, and he and Jonathan said goodbye to each other. It was their last farewell.

David's Wanderings

For several years after that David wandered in the hills with a band of loyal followers, leading a life like Robin Hood's. Sometimes he and his men fought against neighboring tribes that were hostile to the Hebrews. Sometimes they made raids against the Philistines. Most of the time they were busy evading Saul who was trying to find David. Once David came upon Saul as he lay asleep and cut off a piece of his cloak. Later, when Saul awoke, David called to him from a place of hiding and told him how he had been spared. A second time David had a chance to kill Saul and refused it. And once, according to legend, Saul almost stumbled upon David, who was sleeping in a cave. But a spider quickly wove her web across the cave's entrance so that Saul was convinced the cave was empty.

David with the Philistines

Weary of Saul's pursuit, David finally did a surprising thing. He went to Philistia with his followers and sought sanctuary with those traditional enemies of his people. Achish, the ruler of Gath, received him graciously. David swore allegiance to this Philistine king and soon won his favor so completely that Achish gave him a Philistine city to rule over. For several years David and his men lived in Philistia and served Achish.

All of them not only lived comfortably during this time but became acquainted with many refinements of art and civilization that were new to them. David especially, the poet and singer, must have learned much that would make his songs and psalms even more beautiful.

The Death of Saul and Jonathan

The day came when the Philistine armies again marched against the Hebrews in Judah. Achish did not ask David and his men to march with him, and so David was still in Philistia when he heard of the great battle between the Hebrews and the Philistines at Mount Gilboa. In this battle Saul was killed and so were three of his sons, including Jonathan.

The messenger who brought David this news expected him to rejoice that his ancient enemy was dead at last. But David grieved that Judah was vanquished, and he poured out his sorrow over the deaths of Saul and Jonathan in a song of lamentation.

"The beauty of Israel is slain upon thy high places: how are the mighty fallen!" David sang. "Tell it not in Gath, publish it not in the streets of

Askelon, lest the daughters of the Philistines rejoice. . . . Saul and Jonathan were lovely and pleasant in their lives," he sang, "and in their death they were not divided: they were swifter than eagles, they were stronger than lions."

David as King

Still, Saul's death gave David his opportunity. With the encouragement of Achish, who wanted him to be a sort of puppet king in Judah, David went with his men to Hebron in that country and was anointed king of Judah. For more than seven years he ruled there, keeping an uneasy peace with Philistia and battling with a Hebrew general named Abner who wanted to keep the ten tribes of the north for Saul's surviving son.

Then Abner transferred his allegiance to David. Saul's son was killed by his own men, and the elders of the tribes of Israel asked David to be their king also.

David was now king of all the twelve tribes of Hebrews, the ten tribes of Israel and the two of Judah. With this united country behind him, he rallied his army to throw off the domination of Philistia completely. Many battles were fought and there was much bloodshed. But with David's chief general, Joab, leading the Israelite forces, it was finally accomplished. Jerusalem, the Philistine fortress on Mount Zion midway between Judah and the Israelite tribes to the north, was captured. This city was chosen by David to be his capital.

With Israel united and free of Philistia, David and his general, Joab, went on to subdue neighboring countries to the east and north. Finally, under David's rule, Israel became the most powerful country between the Nile and the Euphrates. At last it really seemed to be the Promised Land that Hebrew prophets had predicted for the twelve tribes since the beginning of their history.

Jerusalem, the Royal City

David built his palace in Jerusalem and began to transform the old fortress into a fine city. He ordered the ark of the covenant to be brought to Jerusalem. This was a sacred box, richly inlaid with gold, about which, or in which, the spirit of the God of Israel hovered. Through all the years when the tribes of Israel were wandering or disunited, it had been in hiding. David planned to build a splendid temple for the ark in Jerusalem and made many preparations, but this was a project he was never able to complete.

David and Bathsheba

When most of his battles were over David committed the great mistake of his life. He fell in love with a beautiful woman named Bathsheba who was the wife of one of his generals, Uriah. Desiring to marry Bathsheba, he ordered Uriah to the front in some border warfare in the hope that Uriah would be killed. His hope was fulfilled. Uriah was killed. David soon made Bathsheba his wife. But the Bible tells of how the Lord was angered by this behavior of David's and sent him word of His displeasure by the prophet Nathan. David repented, but the first child Bathsheba bore him died. His second child by Bathsheba was the wise and splendid Solomon.

David's Son Absalom

Because David had many wives, as was the custom in his time, he had had many sons before Solomon. Among these his favorite was Absalom. But in his young manhood Absalom plotted against his father. He managed to win the hearts of the ten tribes of the north and then, with an army of these northern men, he rode to Jerusalem to claim the throne. At his coming David fled from the city along with many of his household. In the wilderness the men who were loyal to David gathered around him to prepare to fight Absalom and his men. Even as the battle approached, David told his captains that Absalom should not be harmed.

But Absalom rode a mule into the wilderness where the battle was to be fought. As he rode beneath an oak tree, the branches caught in his long hair. So firmly was his hair tangled in the branches that he was lifted off his mule and held dangling in the air as his mule walked on. Some of David's men found him there. Ignoring David's instructions, they killed the young prince and cast him into a pit.

This brought an end to the revolt of the northern tribes, and David was soon established in Jerusalem again. But his anger at the men who had killed

his son was great, and his grief for Absalom overwhelmed him. The words of his lamentation have echoed down the centuries.

"O my son Absalom, my son, my son Absalom! Would God I had died for thee!"

David's Death

There were more plots, more battles, a plague, and many other happenings during David's long reign as king of Israel. But at last he grew old.

A Jewish legend tells that there had been a prophecy that David would die on the Sabbath day. Since there was also a belief in Israel that the Angel of Death could not come near anyone while he was studying the law of God, David spent every Sabbath in study. One Sabbath, however, he chanced to hear a noise in the garden. For a moment he left his books and stepped out into the garden. And there the Angel of Death found him, and struck him dead to the ground.

Then Solomon, his youngest son, to whom he had willed the kingdom, called great eagles from the sky to stand about his father's body and protect it until the next day when he could be buried.

7
King Arthur and His Round Table

KING ARTHUR was knighthood's king.

The stories about him tell us that he was a king of England during the Middle Ages and that it was he who introduced the manners and customs of chivalry to that land. Before his time—according to the stories—Englishmen spent most of their time fighting each other for any sort of cause, or even none at all. Highway robbery, kidnapping, murder, all kinds of lawless behavior were taken for granted.

And then came Arthur who summoned the knights of his kingdom to meet around a great Round Table. He urged them to help him put an end to the senseless fighting and cruelty and to use their energies in helping people instead. If they wanted to fight, let them fight to protect those who were weaker than they and to rescue anyone in trouble. The knights swore to follow these new ideals and rode forth in quest of brave and noble deeds to do. And so the idea of chivalry was born and spread from England to France and then all over Europe.

At least, that is what the stories say.

The Real King Arthur

Actually there was no King Arthur in England during the Middle Ages. Long before, in the sixth century, in what we call the Dark Ages—after the Roman Empire had crumbled and most Roman colonists had left England— native Britons had a chieftain named Arthur. Almost all that is known surely about him is that he was a powerful leader who rallied the Celtic tribes of

northern England to resist the settlement in the south of Saxon invaders from the European continent. He must have been an inspiring man for he soon became a hero of folklore. Through the years, and then through the centuries, people told each other stories about the valiant Arthur, giving him credit for all sorts of brave deeds, making him the focal figure of almost any exciting story about warfare or magic or romance.

Finally, about the beginning of the Middle Ages, in the twelfth century, a man named Geoffrey of Monmouth wrote down what he called the history of Arthur. It was a hodgepodge of all the tales and legends that had accumulated over the years around Arthur's name, but most people accepted the account as true. About the same time a writer in France, where Arthur's legends were also popular, used Arthur as the hero of a long romance. Soon other chroniclers in both France and England were writing their versions of the Arthur story.

Then, in 1470, when the Middle Ages were almost over, Sir Thomas Malory in England wrote out the whole story once again, changing it and rearranging it to make it as exciting and beautiful as he could. Malory set the story in the early Middle Ages and he made Arthur the father of chivalry.

Malory's version of the Arthur story, called *Morte d'Arthur,* became the most famous of them all. His is the version on which poets and novelists have based their retellings of the legend through the years since. His is the one in which we see Arthur in the midst of the beauty, cruelty, mystery, and magic that seem to symbolize the Middle Ages.

The Legend of How He Became King

Malory's *Morte d'Arthur* begins with the birth of a son to King Uther Pendragon of England. Unhappily, there was so much jealousy and treachery at Camelot, the king's court, that the king's advisor, a magician named Merlin (who could see the future), counseled the king to send the baby away to be raised secretly.

So young Arthur grew to boyhood in the castle of a poor but worthy knight, Sir Ector. Arthur thought that he was Sir Ector's son and that Sir Ector's older son, Kay, was his brother. The years passed. King Uther Pendragon died, and it seemed that he had not left an heir. Various knights pressed their claims to be the next king. All over the kingdom there was uneasiness as people wondered who would be their next ruler. But there was still no hint that an obscure boy named Arthur in the castle of an obscure knight, Sir Ector, might have anything to do with the problem.

Then, one day, Sir Ector decided to attend a tournament that was being held at Camelot and to take Kay and Arthur with him. They had already ridden some way from home when Kay discovered that he had forgotten his sword. He asked Arthur to ride back and get it for him.

Arthur was used to doing errands for his brother and started off cheerfully. But as he rode toward home he could not help being sorry that he would miss the beginning of the tournament.

Just then he looked toward the churchyard which he was passing and saw what seemed to be a beautiful sword thrust into a stone.

It was an unusual place to see a sword, but Arthur did not stop to wonder how it had come there. Thinking only how fortunate it was that he had found a sword without going all the way home, he got off his horse and ran toward it. He took hold of the sword's hilt, pulled, and the sword slipped out of the stone easily. Pleased, he hurried back to his horse and rode after Sir Ector and Kay.

He caught up with Kay first and handed him the sword. But suddenly Kay noticed some lettering on the hilt of the sword. Kay stared. Then he rode quickly to his father.

"Look," Kay said. "Look at the sword I have." He handed it to his father. Sir Ector looked at the lettering on the hilt, and it was his turn to stare.

Whoso draweth me from the stone is rightwise king of England, the lettering read.

Sir Ector looked up at Kay. "Did you draw this sword from the stone yourself?" he asked.

Kay was not a dishonest boy. He only hesitated a moment and then said, "No. Arthur brought it to me."

Sir Ector turned to Arthur. "Where did you get this sword?" he asked.

"I drew it from the stone in the churchyard," said Arthur.

"You alone?" asked Sir Ector.

"Of course," answered Arthur, feeling puzzled.

Then he was suddenly frightened for Sir Ector was kneeling on the ground before him and pulling Kay to his knees also.

"I give you my homage, sire," Sir Ector was saying.

"What are you doing, father?" cried Arthur. "What are you saying? Get up. I am no one to kneel to. I am just your son Arthur."

"No," said Sir Ector. "I see that the time has come to tell you that you are not really my son. You were brought to me when you were a baby by Merlin, the magician. He told me only that you were of noble birth and that I was to raise you as my own until the time came for your true identity to be revealed. And that is now. By drawing this sword from the stone in the churchyard you have proved you are Uther Pendragon's son and, as such, the new king of England."

The knights gathered at Camelot for the tournament were not so easy to convince as Sir Ector. There was an uproar when Sir Ector showed them the sword and told them that Arthur had drawn it from the stone in the church-yard and that it was all part of a miracle designed to solve the problem of who would next be king. The knights insisted on riding to the churchyard, putting the sword back in the stone, and then allowing everyone a chance to pull it out.

But once the sword was thrust back into the stone not one of the knights could budge it. Only Arthur could draw it out. Still there were arguments among the knights, and finally it was decided to refer the matter to the Archbishop who was head of the church in England. The Archbishop realized that everyone in the country must be convinced that Arthur was indeed the only person in the kingdom who could move the sword. He suggested that a great contest be held in the spring and that every man who wished be given a chance to try his power.

Knights came from all over England to the churchyard for the contest. One by one, each man tried to draw the sword from the stone. One by one, in the sight of all, each failed. Then Arthur was brought forward. As before, he grasped the hilt of the sword and then drew it out easily.

After that everyone had to admit that Arthur was the one fated by the miracle and was just what the sword proclaimed, "rightwise king of England."

How Arthur Started His Round Table

Arthur still had to spend several years fighting to defend his crown. There were small kingdoms in the west and north of England in those times, and the kings of those kingdoms banded together to try to take Arthur's throne from him.

Arthur grew to hate war during these years. He had his father's old advisor, Merlin the magician, by his side now, and he talked to Merlin about it, asking the magician if there were not some way that men could be cured of the fever of wanting to fight. The battles with the jealous kings were finally over and Arthur won peace. But with men always so eager to fight for any sort of reason, Arthur wondered how long he could make the peace last. Soon somebody would start a new war just for something to do.

For a while he forgot his worries when he fell in love with a beautiful princess named Guinevere, who was the daughter of a friendly king of a neighboring kingdom. No difficulties spoiled the romance. Soon Arthur and Guinevere were married with much pomp and ceremony. Among the wedding presents Guinevere's father sent to the couple was an enormous round table.

Suddenly, as he looked at the table Arthur had an inspiration. He thought of a plan that just might give the knights of his kingdom something more interesting to do than persist in making war.

Arthur sent out an invitation to all the best knights of England to join him at Camelot. When they arrived, he sat them down around the huge table. Then he asked them to think and talk about how they could use their knightly skills without starting wars. Once the knights really understood what the king was talking about they realized that they could use their strength in many ways. One by one they vowed to fight only in worthy causes. Then a special seat was set aside for each man sworn as a knight of the Round Table, to be his place whenever he returned to Camelot.

Some stories about King Arthur say that there were one thousand seats at his Round Table. Malory wrote that there were only one hundred and fifty, of which one hundred and thirty were filled at the beginning while twenty were left vacant for knights who might prove themselves worthy. Whichever legend one likes to believe, there were certainly enough seats so that a great many knights were soon riding about England, looking for wrongs to right, poor people to help, maidens to rescue, and dragons to slay. And when all of them came back to Camelot they had many exciting adventures to relate.

Before long, still another mission became one of the goals of the knights of the Round Table. This, the noblest mission on which any knight could embark, was a search for the Holy Grail, which was what men called the cup used by Jesus at the Last Supper. The cup was, of course, many centuries old by this time, but men were sure it existed somewhere and could be found by someone. But legend said it could only be found by a knight who was absolutely pure in heart, without fear and without reproach. Many of King Arthur's knights rode out in quest of the Grail. One found it—Sir Galahad. His adventures fill many pages of Malory's story about King Arthur.

Sir Lancelot, who was Galahad's father, also played a very important role in Malory's story. He was a knight who had come from France to join the Round Table, and he became the greatest warrior of them all as well as King Arthur's best friend.

Other knights whose stories were told in Malory's long book include Tristan, who had a tragic romance with a lady named Isolde; Bedivere, who was the king's steward; Gawain, Gareth, Percival, Bors, Balan, and the king's nephew, Mordred.

Excalibur and the Death of Arthur

All the stories and legends about King Arthur agree that he had a sword called Excalibur which had a jeweled hilt and magic powers to protect its owner. Some of the legends say that it was the same sword that young Arthur drew from the stone. Other versions of the story describe it as a different sword and tell a strange tale about how Arthur acquired it.

Arthur and Merlin were riding in the woods one day—these stories say—and passed by a lake. A woman's voice suddenly called to the king. The king looked toward the lake, which was in the direction from which the voice seemed to call. In the center of the lake there rose from the water an arm draped in samite (a heavy silk), and the hand of the arm held a sword. Near the edge of the lake a beautiful lady suddenly appeared, shadowy and phantomlike. The phantom lady spoke and said that she was the Lady of the Lake. She offered the king the magic sword in exchange for his promise that if she ever asked a favor of him he would grant it. Arthur gave his promise to do so. The Lady of the Lake then pointed to a barge at the lake's edge and told the king to row out and take the sword. Arthur did so. As he grasped the sword the mysterious arm disappeared and so did the phantom lady.

After that, Arthur always carried the sword Excalibur. A time came when the Lady of the Lake asked a favor of him as she had promised, and this led to strange and wonderful adventure for King Arthur.

Malory's story about King Arthur makes it clear that for a while some of the things Arthur hoped to achieve with his Round Table did come to pass. With his knights setting an example, people became less warlike and more interested in fighting for worthy causes.

But wickedness and cruelty did not end. There were quarrels even at the Round Table. Finally, some really bad trouble was started by Sir Mordred, Arthur's nephew. Mordred hated his uncle from the moment he came to Arthur's court and plotted to spoil the King's plans whenever he could. At last Mordred found an opportunity to set Sir Lancelot and the king against each other. Neither Lancelot nor Arthur wanted to quarrel but Mordred plotted so cleverly and whispered so many scandals that soon the knights of the Round Table were divided into two factions—those for the king and those for Lancelot.

The trouble grew until at last Lancelot and his followers fled to France. King Arthur and his men pursued them and soon were besieging the castle in which they had taken refuge. Then word came from England that Sir Mordred was plotting to kidnap Queen Guinevere in their absence. Both Arthur and Lancelot quit fighting each other at this news and hurried back to England.

In the battle against Mordred that followed, King Arthur received a mortal wound. As he lay dying, he did not grieve for himself. He was old and tired. But he did grieve because it seemed to him that all that he had struggled for had been destroyed. The knights of his Round Table were fighting each other. Many were dead. The ideal of fighting only for right and justice and to protect the weak seemed to have vanished.

Arthur called his steward, Sir Bedivere. He gave Bedivere his sword, Excalibur, and told him to take it back to the lake from which he had received it long ago and to throw it in the water there. Soon after that he died. Or so some stories say.

Malory's story tells us that as Arthur lay at the point of death the old magician, Merlin, appeared, accompanied by three fairy queens. The fairy queens lifted Arthur, carried him to a barge, and rowed him to the magical island of Avalon, where he would not die. Instead he would live on, in a fairy world, until some time in the distant future when England would have need of him again, and he would return to serve the country as before.

So Malory's story left the King Arthur legend without an ending—only an interruption, until once again Arthur would be summoned to encourage men to knightly ideals.

8
Charlemagne

CHARLEMAGNE was a majestic figure with a mane of white hair and a beard like a snowdrift. He sat on a golden throne with his twelve peers, or paladins, around him. Or he rode into battle on a beautiful white horse, followed by his paladins.

This picture of Charlemagne comes from legend, story, and song, particularly from a long poem called *The Song of Roland,* which was as popular during the Middle Ages as the legends about King Arthur. But unlike Arthur, Charlemagne was a very real king, and the events and achievements of his life are part of history.

King of the Franks

Charles, who later became known as the Great, was born about A.D. 742. He was a Frank, one of the Frankish people who lived across a wide area of western Europe, which was divided into many little kingdoms, states, or clans. His grandfather, Charles Martel, or Charles the Hammer, had taken the first steps in uniting some of those small states into one Frankish kingdom. His father, Pepin the Short, brought still more states and territories under his rule and also fought in Italy, defending Rome against invaders. When Pepin died, he left his kingdom to his two sons, Charles, who was the older, and Carloman. But Carloman died in 771, and Charles became sole king of the Franks.

From then on, Charles did even more than his father and grandfather had done to unite the people of western Europe under one ruler. He brought more Frankish territory under his rule. He fought the Germanic tribes east of the Rhine River and brought them into his kingdom. He even marched far southeastward into the territory of the Slavs and made conquests there.

Because he was a Christian, as his father and grandfather had been, he fought as much for his religion as he did for empire. He forced the pagan Germans—and all other pagans whom he conquered—to convert to Christianity. And whenever Christendom seemed threatened he hurried to the rescue. He invaded Spain hoping to overthrow the Mohammedan rule of the Moors there. He was defeated by the Moors at Saragossa but still managed to hold a few Spanish cities and to set up a fortified watch along the Spanish border to guard against any invasion of his kingdom by Mohammedans. And when the pope in Rome suddenly found himself in difficulties, Charles took his armies to Rome to support and defend him.

The Holy Roman Empire

By then it was 799. Charles had extended his kingdom to cover an area almost as large as the Roman Empire once had been. What was more, it was a Christian empire, thanks to Charles's efforts. It seemed logical to the grateful pope, and to almost everyone else as well, that this empire should be recognized as the Roman Empire revived, or re-created. On Christmas Day, A.D. 800, the pope crowned Charles emperor of this vast domain, calling it the Holy Roman Empire.

The need to battle continued. The Germanic tribes were not completely subdued until 804. Soon after that the first of the viking raiders from Norway and Denmark began harassing the French coast, and Charles had to lead his armies to deal with them.

In spite of all the warfare, however, Charles's reign and the creation of the Holy Roman Empire really marked the beginning of the end of the Dark Ages, when barbarians from the east were overrunning Europe. Charles did more than win battles. He was a wise and thoughtful ruler. He had laws written down throughout his empire. He organized its administration so that he could keep in touch with what was going on everywhere. His court was in Aachen, and he made that city an intellectual center to which he summoned scholars from all over Europe. He established a famous school in Aachen and had other schools started all over the land. He was interested in the great works of classical times and arranged for them to be studied and preserved. He encouraged art, music, and all the refinements of civilization.

Charles the Great he was called, and with reason, or Charles Magnus (the Latin word *magnus* meaning great) , which in French became Charlemagne.

Charlemagne's Death

Charlemagne died, aged seventy-two, in 814. After his death, his son Louis became emperor. But Louis was not the brilliant leader that his father had been, and the powerful empire gradually became weaker. Then Louis divided it into several parts so that all his sons might have kingdoms, and this further undermined Charlemagne's creation.

Charlemagne's Fame

It was a long time before any of Charlemagne's successors matched him in wisdom and power. As a result, people began to think of him as the ideal of a Christian emperor. In Germany he was claimed as the ancestor of a whole line of German kings and canonized in 1165. France also claimed him as her greatest king in the Carlovingian dynasty (named for its founder, Charles the Hammer) . Everywhere in Europe, he became a figure of legend, growing more magnificent and good as the stories about him were told and retold by poets, singers, and troubadors.

The Song of Roland

The chief character of the famous story-poem *The Song of Roland* is a fictional nephew of Charlemagne's. Roland is shown first as a boy, living in poverty with his mother, Charlemagne's sister, unaware of his relationship to the emperor. The boy was happy, in spite of being poor, and played at being a knight with a good friend, Oliver, the son of a nobleman who lived nearby.

Then Charlemagne rode into the story, his paladins around him. The great emperor camped in a valley not far from where Roland and his mother were living. The boy was so excited that his mother decided to tell him that Charlemagne was her brother but had banished her from his court when she made a marriage that displeased him. Roland's vision of the emperor as a good and generous man vanished. He was outraged by what seemed harsh and cruel treatment of his mother. He ran to Charlemagne's camp and made his way past all the guards to the emperor to demand the best food and drink from his table for his mother. At first the boy's audacity amused Charlemagne, but then it was revealed that the boy's mother was the emperor's sister. Charlemagne's mood changed. He had long since regretted his treatment of his sister. He embraced the boy whom he recognized as his nephew and sent at once for Roland's mother so that she and the boy both might take their proper places in his court.

The Great Sword Durendal and the Ivory Horn

The Roland poem tells how Roland and his mother rode away with Charlemagne and his host the very next day, so quickly that Roland had no chance to say good-by to his friend, Oliver. And of how, during the years that followed, Roland learned all the knightly skills at Charlemagne's court. When it was time for his knighting, Charlemagne gave him a beautiful sword, called Durendal, which was supposed to have belonged to Hector, the Greek hero of the Trojan War. Another prize Roland won from his uncle was an ivory horn that had belonged to Charles the Hammer (Charlemagne's grandfather). Such strength was needed to blow the horn that no one since Charles the Hammer had been able to raise a sound from it. When Roland blew it and made the echoes ring, Charlemagne gave it to him but told him never to blow the horn except in time of utmost need.

A Roland for an Oliver

Roland was soon recognized as the finest knight in Charlemagne's army. One time Charlemagne and his soldiers were pressing a siege against a rebellious nobleman. An offer came from the nobleman inside the castle under siege that the issue be decided by two knights fighting in single combat. The nobleman had a champion whom he would send to meet any champion that Charlemagne should select. Roland was chosen to fight the unknown champion.

The two knights rode toward each other and fought fiercely. But it was soon plain that they were wonderfully evenly matched. Both were unhorsed at the same time. The swords of both broke at the same time. They lifted their visors to run at each other and continue the battle on foot. But as soon

as they had a clear view of each other they stopped and then ran to shake hands. Roland had recognized the unknown champion as Oliver, the friend of his childhood. And Oliver had recognized Roland.

With the two opposing champions renewing their vows of friendship, Charlemagne soon came to terms with the rebelling nobleman. After this, Oliver became one of Charlemagne's knights, and he and Roland were inseparable companions. As a result, the phrase "a Roland for an Oliver" has come to mean two friends, equally talented, who cannot defeat each other but together can defeat all challengers.

The Battle with the Saracens

Charlemagne's actual, historical battles with the Moors in Spain (who, like all Mohammedans, were called Saracens by the Europeans) were dramatized in *The Song of Roland*.

The poem tells of how Roland and Oliver fought more valiantly than any other knights in Spain, spreading terror among the forces of the Saracen king, Marsilius. Finally, a truce was agreed on. Then one of Charlemagne's peers, a nobleman named Ganelon, who had been jealous of Roland since he first came to court, had a secret meeting with Marsilius. Ganelon told the Saracen king of a plan whereby he could revenge himself on Roland, and whereby he, Ganelon, might also end Roland's influence on Charlemagne forever. In exchange for a certain sum of gold, Ganelon promised Marsilius that when Charlemagne's armies went back across the mountains to France Roland would be leading the rear guard. In return, Marsilius promised that he would have a thousand men waiting in ambush at a narrow pass in the mountains called Roncesvalles.

Charlemagne and his army began their march toward home. Roland, with Oliver beside him, was leading the rear guard, just as Ganelon had promised. The main part of the army was far ahead when the rear guard came to the pass at Roncesvalles.

The Saracens sprang out of ambush—a thousand men to the hundred that made up the rear guard. The situation looked so hopeless for the French that Oliver urged Roland to blow his ivory horn. But Roland was too proud to call for help. So he, Oliver, and the rest of the guard rode at their attackers, their swords flashing.

Brave as the French knights were, they were no match for a thousand Saracens. More than half of Roland's rear guard had fallen when Roland saw that Oliver was wounded. Then, at last, he raised the ivory horn to blow a call for help to Charlemagne.

The sound of the horn carried over the mountains. Charlemagne, riding at the head of his host, heard it and knew Roland was blowing the ivory horn in a call for help. Ganelon, who rode beside him, tried to persuade the king that Roland was blowing the horn for sport, but Charlemagne was sure Roland was only blowing it in utmost need. He ordered the army to turn back and ride as fast as it could toward Roncesvalles.

Even so, Charlemagne and his men arrived at the pass too late. Oliver was dead. Roland also was slain. Charlemagne found him lying with his bright sword, Durendal, beside him, the ivory horn still in his hands.

Charlemagne grieved for Roland and Oliver as he had grieved for no other knights fallen in battle. He learned, finally, that Ganelon had been responsible for their deaths and Ganelon was punished. With Ganelon's death, *The Song of Roland* came to its end.

9
Alfred the Great

The Story of the Cakes

One winter's night a stranger came to the door of a poor cowherder's cottage seeking shelter. He told the cowherder and his wife that he was one of King Alfred's men, making his way home after the summer's battles with the Danes but so exhausted that he had to rest for several days before going on.

The cowherder and his wife were glad to do what they could for the weary stranger. Their cottage was far inland from the Wessex coast where the Danes did most of their raiding, but they had heard many stories about the cruelty of the Danish invaders. The knew King Alfred and his men fought against them year after year, trying to drive them out of England for good, so they felt that they were helping in the fight by helping one of his soldiers.

But when day followed day and the stranger stayed on, the cowherder's wife began to wonder about him. He was rested enough to travel. Many days he left the cottage in the morning, but he always returned at nightfall. Where he went he never said. When he was in the cottage he generally sat near the fire, staring at the flames and brooding. The cowherder's wife grew more and more impatient with him.

She was very busy one morning, with tasks to do outside the cottage as well as indoors. Putting some oatcakes over the fire to bake, she spoke to the stranger who was sitting watching the fire as always.

"Will you keep an eye on the cakes for me, please," she asked, "and take them off the fire when they are brown?"

The stranger nodded. Relieved, the woman went outside to do her chores there.

But the room was full of a smell of burning food when she came in an hour or so later. She looked toward the hearth. The pan of oatcakes was still on the

fire. The cakes were black as cinders. And there sat the stranger, just as she had left him, staring straight at the fire and letting the cakes burn.

"Oh, what a good for nothing!" cried the woman, losing her temper. "You are glad enough to eat the cakes when they are set before you, but you cannot trouble yourself for a minute to keep them from burning."

The stranger seemed to wake from a dream as she scolded. He started to apologize, but she would not listen.

"Who do you think you are?" she cried. "The king himself?" Then, paying no more attention to him, she busied herself in making a fresh batch of cakes. She had no idea that she had just guessed her visitor's identity exactly. The stranger who lingered on and on was indeed King Alfred himself, hiding in the cowherder's cottage through the winter while he planned a new, surprise attack on the Danes to take place in the spring.

This, one of the most famous of all legends about King Alfred of England, leaves just one bothersome little question unanswered. Did the cowherder's wife ever find out that she had been sheltering a king? Did he tell her when he left in the spring, so that she could apologize for scolding him? Or did she learn much later that she had set a king to watch her oatcakes?

There are other legends about Alfred. One tells of how he once disguised himself as a harpist so that he could make his way into a Danish encampment and overhear the enemy's plans. But even though historians do not accept legends like these as fact, Alfred was not a legendary king, as King Arthur of the Round Table was, but a very real one. The true story of what he actually did do for England is more exciting than any legend.

England in Alfred's Times

Alfred was born in A.D. 849, at Wantage, in the southern part of England where the Saxons had been established for almost four centuries. He was the fourth and youngest son of Ethelwulf, king of Wessex, which was the region where the West Saxons lived. His older brothers were named Ethelbald, Ethelbert, and Ethelred ("ethel" meant "noble" in the Saxon language).

The time of Alfred's birth, not quite fifty years after Charlemagne's reign in France, was just a year or so before Harold Fairhair became King of Norway. The vikings of Harold's Norse kingdom and the vikings of Denmark had become the terror of all Europe. Sailing their dragon ships, these vikings were raiding and pirating in all directions. They voyaged eastward across the Baltic and down the rivers of Russia. They sailed southwestward down the coast of Europe as far as Spain and then into the Mediterranean and beyond. But England, not far away and directly westward from Denmark, was a special target for Danish vikings.

For almost thirty years before Alfred was born the Danes had been appearing off the English coast every summer, to land and then loot, burn, pillage, and murder. Once in a while the Saxons along the coast were able to unite and fight back against the invaders. One famous viking, Ragnar Lodbrok, who fought under a raven banner, had been killed by the resisting Saxons. But generally the Danes were stronger, and gradually they became more and more bold. They learned to "horse themselves" as soon as they touched shore so that they could move as freely on land as they could on the sea, and this made them even more dangerous. When Alfred was still a baby, a great band of Danes camped all winter near the mouth of the Thames River and then, when spring came, they plundered London.

One after another, the little kingdoms in the eastern part of England were captured by the Danish raiders. Wessex, farther west, had not been attacked yet, but the Saxons there lived in fear that their turn would soon come.

Still, in spite of the Danish threat, when Alfred was five years old his father sent him, along with a proper escort of servants and soldiers, on a pilgrimage to Rome. Rome, a city which had suffered many difficulties from the third century on, was once again the center of European civilization and had also become the headquarters of the Christian church in the West. Young Alfred saw the great buildings of antiquity, was presented to important people, and was blessed by the Pope before returning to England. Two years later, his father again took him to Rome.

This time when they returned to England they found the Danes were closer to Wessex than ever before, and with each raid they came nearer. The next years brought other troubles as well. Alfred's father died. Then, one by one, as Alfred's brothers succeeded their father, they died, until Ethelred, the brother next older to Alfred, was king.

The Battle of Ashdown

It was 866 and Alfred was seventeen when the Danes at last made a full-scale attack on Wessex. Ethelred rallied his army, and Alfred fought at his side in a series of battles and skirmishes that went on until 871. In that year the Saxons finally managed to defeat the Danes in the famous battle of Ashdown. The Danes now felt such a healthy respect for the West Saxons that they retreated to the north and east of England and left Wessex alone for a while.

Alfred Becomes King

King Ethelred died the same year that the Danes were defeated, and Alfred became king of Wessex at the age of twenty-two.

He had been married since 868 to a daughter of the king of Mercia, which was one of the little kingdoms in eastern England that the Danes had captured. Soon after his marriage, Alfred suffered some strange sort of illness. No records give any clue as to just what was wrong, but he was not really strong for the rest of his life. This did not prevent him from striving valiantly, year after year, for the welfare of his kingdom.

In 875, the Danes had forgotten their fear of Wessex men enough to begin their raids again. Alfred gathered his men and went out to meet them. For two years, the Saxons fought the Danes on land and on the sea, too, as well as they could.

Then a great storm wrecked a hundred and more Danish ships off the Wessex coast, and Alfred and his men relaxed their guard. The Danes took advantage of this Saxon carelessness. Led by their chief, Guthrun, they attacked in force.

Alfred and his Saxons were defeated so badly in this battle that they retreated into the marshes of Athelney in Somerset, scattering and going into hiding. And it was during the winter that followed that Alfred took refuge with the cowherder, according to legend, and let the oatcakes burn.

Wherever he stayed during that winter, he was meeting secretly with his soldiers from time to time. When the circumstances were right, they made swift guerrilla attacks on the Danish camps beyond the marshes. Mostly, they waited and planned for spring.

When the weather warmed, Alfred's soldiers gathered about him. Then, in a quick forced march, Alfred and his men made their way to the main Danish camp at Edington, where Guthrun was established. The surprise attack by

the Saxons brought on fierce Danish resistance. But this time the Saxons, encouraged and inspired by Alfred, could not be pushed back. At the end of two weeks, Guthrun and his men surrendered to Alfred.

One of Alfred's terms for the surrender was that the Danes, still pagans, should accept Christianity. This demand, like all the others, was accepted. A few days later, the whole Danish army was baptized by Alfred's priests. Alfred himself stood as godfather for Guthrun when he accepted Christianity.

After that, the Danes retreated northward and eastward, toward the strip of land along the eastern coast of England which Alfred had granted them. This eastern area of England became known as the Danelaw, since it was under Danish control and remained so for more than a hundred years.

Now and then, for the rest of his reign, Alfred had some trouble with Danes who could not resist raiding along the borders of their Danelaw. But never again were there battles like the one that sent Alfred into hiding or the one where he was victorious at Edington.

Rebuilding Wessex

With the Danes more or less checked, Alfred was able to devote himself to restoring his kingdom. Wessex showed all the effects of years of terror and fighting. Almost no one had had time to read or study during the years of fear. Children had grown up unlettered. There were no scholars and no books. Life in general was primitive and disorganized. Alfred set himself to changing all that.

He had the laws of the kingdom written down, and he set up a system of government administration. He rebuilt monasteries as libraries and centers for studies and imported scholars from Europe to staff them. He began the keeping of the *Anglo-Saxon Chronicle,* the first historical record ever attempted in England. He founded the first public schools in England, where the sons of noblemen and thanes could study reading, writing, and other useful subjects.

Alfred's mother had taught him to read when he was young, but he had learned Saxon only. Now that he was grown, he taught himself Latin, the language of the church and of scholarship. Then he began to make his own contribution to the civilization of Wessex, translating books of theology, history, and geography from Latin into Anglo-Saxon.

All these efforts to bring order and learning to Wessex did not cause Alfred to overlook the need for constant military preparedness. He set up a system for recruiting an army when needed and arranged for permanent garrisons in strategic forts. And, learning a lesson from the past when the Danes in their swift ships raided the English coast as they pleased, he began building up a naval fleet for his country.

King of All England

Alfred was really only king of Wessex, a southwestern corner of England, but by 886, Saxons all over England were thinking of him as their king. Even the Danes of the Danelaw felt a special reverence for this brave, busy ruler who was concerned about every aspect of his subjects' welfare. Because of the love and loyalty that he inspired all over England, Alfred is the first English king who can be called king of England, not just one of its provinces.

Even before his death in 899, Alfred had won a special place in the history of his country. In the centuries since his death men have given him many loving and grateful names—Shepherd of the English, the Good, Gray King— but one name remains secure. He was, and will always be, Alfred the Great.

10

King Canute

Canute and the Waves

King Canute was riding along an ocean shore in England with a group of his courtiers. He was asking their advice as to whether or not he should attempt some particularly difficult undertaking. The courtiers hardly seemed to listen as he spoke of the problems in detail. Their main concern was to assure him that nothing was too difficult for him to do. Thinking only of how they could flatter and please him, they told him he was all-powerful. A king in his own country, had he not crossed the North Sea to conquer England and become its king as well? Plainly, such a ruler of land and sea could do anything he wished.

Suddenly King Canute checked his horse. His followers quickly halted their mounts also.

"You say I rule the seas," said Canute.

"Yes, of course," said one of the men. All the others nodded and agreed.

The king looked out toward the ocean. He noticed that the tide was completely out and just beginning to turn. He looked back at his men.

"Come with me," said King Canute. He dismounted and walked down the beach. Puzzled, his men followed him.

Canute reached the line of seaweed and pebbles that marked the high-tide line of the water. He walked beyond it onto the firmer sand closer to the water. He faced the water and raised his hand in a commanding gesture.

"Halt!" he cried to the water. "Come not an inch farther."

The waves continued to break as before, each one just a little farther up the shore than the one before.

"Halt!" said Canute again. "I am the all-powerful king, ruler of the lands

of the north and the seas of the north. I command you, sea, as your ruler. Come no farther."

A wave broke at his feet. The men with him began to move back up the beach. "Sire," they cried. "Step back. You will be drenched."

The king paid no heed. He called out again to the water. "Halt!"

A great wave rolled in, broke, and then the water swirled around the king's knees, and the spray flew up about him, almost hiding him from sight.

"Your majesty!" cried his men, running to rescue him. Canute let them lead him to firmer sand beyond the reach of the water.

"Why did you do such a dangerous thing?" asked one of the men. "You know that the tide here can draw a man into deeper water in a moment. You could have drowned. Why did you do it?"

"So, I have to spell out the lesson?" said Canute. "Very well, I will. I wanted to show you plainly that there is a limit to my power as there is to every man's. Now when I ask your advice, let me have reasonable responses that recognize that fact. Let there be no more foolish talk about Canute being all-powerful."

Canute, the Danish King of England

Canute, who was born in A.D. 995 and lived until 1035, was the first Danish king of England. He came onto the scene a hundred and fifty years after Alfred the Great had repulsed the Danes from Wessex and forced the Danes already in England to confine themselves to that section known as the Danelaw. For a long while after Alfred's death, Danish vikings had not troubled England very much. A regular tribute, called Danegeld, was paid to them by the English and in exchange, the vikings did most of their raiding elsewhere. The Danes who had settled in England, in the Danelaw, began to think of England as their home.

But then, toward the end of the tenth century, the vikings of Denmark began remembering England and realizing that if they could capture Wessex they would control most of the country.

The king of Denmark, Sweyn Forkbeard, along with his son Canute, led an expedition against Saxon England. They knew beforehand that they would not have to face anyone like Alfred the Great. One of Alfred's descendants, named Ethelred, was king of Wessex. Men called him Ethelred the

Redeless. In Saxon, "redeless" meant "without advice." And it was true that Ethelred did not have good advisors. In later years, men sometimes recorded "redeless" as "unready." And this nickname was as true as the other. Ethelred was completely unready for an invasion by the Danes. His only idea was to try to buy the Danes off by larger and larger payments of Danegeld. But Sweyn Forkbeard wanted more than just gold. He wanted England.

He led his invaders against the fortified city of London, the gateway to Saxon Wessex. The men of London fought stoutly for their city, but they were no match for the Danes. Soon Sweyn and his vikings had the city and were moving on to Wessex. Ethelred the Unready fled across the English Channel to exile in Normandy.

The Saxon Witan, which was the supreme council of the Saxons, had no choice but to acknowledge Sweyn Forkbeard as king of Wessex. But almost at once Forkbeard died. Ethelred hurried back from Normandy to resume the Wessex crown again, and young Canute, son of Sweyn Forkbeard, sailed home to Denmark.

The next year, however, Canute returned to England with more ships, men, and supplies, determined to try again for Wessex .This time resistance was even weaker. Within a few months, Ethelred the Unready died. His son Edmund Ironsides was named king, but Canute pursued Edmund Ironsides with all his forces. Finally Canute and Edmund Ironsides met at Ashingdon in Essex, and Edmund Ironsides was defeated. Canute's victory won him the control of most of England and when Ironsides died a few months later, Canute became king of all the land—all the England that the Danes held as well as the England over which Alfred the Great had reigned.

Canute's Wisdom

The legend about Canute and the waves reflects the wisdom and good judgment that the young king showed when he took over the English crown.

He did have much power. Soon after becoming king of England, the death of an older brother made him king of Denmark. About ten years later he became king of Norway as well. This made him the ruler of all the most powerful countries in the northern part of Europe. But he used his power constructively, and soon even the Saxons who had fought him were glad to pledge their allegiance to him.

Canute continued to encourage law, order, and learning, as Alfred the Great had done. He erected churches, abbeys, and monasteries.

When he died in 1035 at the early age of forty, he left his Danish and English crowns to his son Hardecanute, but another son, Harold, seized the English crown from his brother and ruled for two years until his death. After that Hardecanute became the third Danish king of England. But neither of Canute's sons had the abilities of their father. By 1042, seven years after Canute's death, a son of Ethelred the Unready had regained the crown for the Saxons.

Canute's Legacy

Canute's reign marked the high point of Danish power in England. And though Danish raids had brought much destruction in earlier years, the settlement of Danes in England brought many good things later. The Danes had their own special talents that mingled with the talents of the Saxons. Seafaring folk by ancestry, the Danes helped to make England the sea power that she later became. And once settled on land, the Danes were also good merchants and traders, clever at building towns and business centers. Their descendants helped to make England a country where businessmen and merchants would play leading roles.

Just thirty-one years after Canute's death, England was again conquered by invaders, this time by invaders from Normandy on the French coast. (See the story of William the Conqueror.) It was a curious twist of fate that these Norman invaders who took over England from both the Saxons and Danes were themselves descendants of Danish vikings who had raided the French coast years and years before, then settled down in France to adopt French ways, laws, and the French language.

11
Henry of Navarre

The White Plume

HENRY IV OF FRANCE was a wise, tolerant, and witty king, who united France after its many years of civil war because of religious differences.

The plume, "the white plume of Navarre," was his symbol. It reminded the world that Henry was a Gascon. The Gascons were descendants of the fiercely independent Basques. An intelligent and industrious people, they lived along the border that now separates Spain and France. Their kingdom, Navarre, was small and mountainous. The mountains made existence difficult, but hardship sharpened the Gascons' wit. It taught them to enjoy the good things of life all the more. A good fight for a good reason, a good joke, good food, good wine, good companions—these were the loves of every Gascon's life. Henry was as much a Gascon as any one person could be. His warmth and charm drew people to him. His courage and integrity kept them at his side. From the mountainsides of Navarre to the very gates of Paris, men rallied to the man who wore the plume. Proudly, they followed Henry across the battlefields of France. "Here is a man one can trust," his white plume seemed to say, "a soldier, yet a man romantic at heart." Henry's men felt the plume spoke for them: "Let the enemy heed the white plume of Navarre."

France in Henry's Time

Henry was born in 1553—not quite forty years after the start of a sort of religious earthquake in Europe. For centuries there had been only one Christian church in the western world—the Catholic Church with its headquarters in Rome. Everyone who called himself a Christian belonged to that church and only thought of fighting a religious war with people who had an entirely different system of belief, like the Mohammedans. And then, suddenly, the earthquake was under way. Many Christians, protesting against abuses of Catholic Church power, which had increased through the years, began withdrawing from what had been the only church and setting up small churches of their own in which they hoped to do away with these abuses. Because theirs was a protest movement they were soon called Protestants. Their actions aroused furious anger in those Christians who remained loyal to the Catholic Church, and the anger quickly led to battle, bloodshed, and death all over Europe.

Henry was exposed to this conflict from the moment of his birth. His father was Antoine de Bourbon, Duke of Vendôme, a member of one of France's noblest families. He was a man who joined with the Protestants for a while, then forswore their beliefs and went back to fight for the Catholic Church. Henry's mother was Jeanne d'Albret, queen of Navarre. She was an ardent Protestant who never dreamed of wavering in her belief and raised her son to be as devoutly Protestant as she.

A Young Soldier

Henry was just sixteen years old when his mother, Queen Jeanne, took him to the leader of the Protestant forces to arrange for his enlistment in the army that was fighting the militant Catholic forces of France. Henry distinguished himself as a soldier in his first battle.

King, Husband, Prisoner of the Catholics

In 1572, Henry's mother died, and he became king of Navarre. Later the same year, he was married to Margaret of Valois who was a sister of the king of France, Charles IX. The wedding took place in Paris, and because by this time Henry was an important and influential Protestant many Protestant leaders came to Paris to be present at the ceremony. This gathering of Protestants in one city triggered a terrible plot among some Catholics of high position. The last war between the two groups was supposed to be over, but a few days after Henry's wedding the Catholics arranged for all the most important Protestants to be killed. This mass killing, which was known as the St.

Bartholomew's Day Massacre, set off further attacks on Protestants all over France. Henry, king of Navarre, was supposed to have been killed with the others but saved his life by forswearing his Protestant beliefs. Even so, he was held as a virtual prisoner in the French court for four years. Finally he managed to escape and when he did he returned to the Protestant faith.

Years of Conflict

The next dozen and more years Henry's life and France's history were filled with more bitter religious warfare. Charles IX, who had wavered between being a Protestant and a Catholic, died and was succeeded by his brother, Henry III, a Catholic. Henry III tried to increase his own power by playing the Catholics and Protestants (or Huguenots as they were called in France) against each other. Then he further complicated matters by naming Henry of Navarre, a Protestant, as his successor. This brought on a three-sided war, involving three Henrys—Henry III, king of France, Henry of Navarre, and Henri de Guise, a Catholic leader who refused to recognize a Protestant as heir to the throne of France. The king of Spain, a devout Catholic, threw his help to Henri de Guise as he fought Henry of Navarre in the War of the Three Henrys.

"Paris Is Worth a Mass"

Mile by mile, Henry of Navarre battled his way toward Paris. Then Henry III, king of France, was killed by a monk who thought he was a danger to France, and Henry of Navarre was presumably the next king. He stood outside the gates of Paris, confident of victory. But years of warfare had deepened his concern for human life. When Paris refused to admit him peacefully, Henry did for France what the French had been unable to do for themselves. He displayed an open mind. He renounced his Protestantism and joined the Catholic Church.

"Paris is worth a Mass," he said, according to legend.

So Henry of Navarre entered Paris and became King Henry IV of France in 1589. The son of Antoine de Bourbon, he was the first of the rulers who became known as the Bourbon kings. He was also a king determined to bring an end to the years of misery, corruption, hunger, and death when everything was forgotten but the bitterness of religious differences.

France Restored

Henry chose good men to carry out his programs. With their help, he reformed finances, ended various abuses, and did away with useless offices. To improve the lot of his people, he developed industry and agriculture. He had marshes drained to make more land available for farming. A complete system of canals was planned to improve transportation. Henry also introduced the silk industry to France, and he encouraged the manufacture of cloth, glassware, and tapestries. The famous Gobelin tapestries are counted among the artistic treasures of France, and many of the most beautiful buildings in present-day Paris were built during Henry's reign.

The Edict of Nantes

Constructive as he was in so many ways, Henry IV's most valuable gift to France was religious peace. In 1598, he forced King Philip II of Spain to make peace with him. In that same year he proclaimed the Edict of Nantes, which granted freedom of worship to all French people. French Huguenots (or Protestants) no longer needed to fear persecution from French Catholics but could openly follow their own interpretation of Christianity.

It was ironic that this king who tried so hard to end religious warfare was stabbed to death in 1610 by a religious fanatic.

Henry's Legends

Henry IV is remembered with affection to this day. Restaurants and places of amusement are named in his honor. His concern for the welfare of his people makes his love of fun all the more appealing. By legend, he was the first to promise the peasants of France "a chicken in every pot every Sunday." The promise sounds like one he might have made. And to it even now, many Frenchmen might reply, "Spoken like a true Gascon."

PART THREE

GREEDY KINGS

"The King was in his counting house
Counting out his money . . ."
MOTHER GOOSE

King Midas

Croesus

Ahab

Henry VIII

12

King Midas

MIDAS had the "golden touch," and almost everyone has heard of him because to him was granted what might seem to be the most fabulous gift in the world—everything he touched turned to gold.

The Midas Legend

According to Greek mythology, Midas was a king of Phrygia. This was one of several countries of ancient times located in what is now Turkey. Its main city was Gordium where was enshrined the wagon tied with the Gordian knot. (See the story of Alexander the Great.)

Midas is said to have lived in the times when the gods of Olympus often walked the earth, and it was because of a favor that he was able to do for the god Bacchus that Midas was granted his marvelous gift.

Bacchus was god of the vine, and hence of the produce of the vine, wine. A son of Zeus, Bacchus had been given as a teacher a fat, merry old man named Silenus. Silenus himself was a sort of demigod—a satyr, or god of the woods, who was half man, half goat. At some point, Bacchus became separated from Silenus, and Midas, King of Phrygia, was able to reunite the two. When Bacchus asked the king what he would like as a reward, Midas answered that he wanted gold—enough to satisfy him forever. He wanted, in fact, the power to make everything he touched turn to gold.

His wish was granted, and for a while King Midas was deliriously happy. He went around touching everything—chairs, tables, clothes, curtains—and he was rapturous when he saw them all transformed into glittering, precious metal. Finally he sat down to eat after all the excitement.

He was pleased to see his water goblet turn to gold as he lifted it to take a drink, but he was disappointed to have the water become solid gold as soon as it touched his lips. He was thirsty. He was pleased to have his knife turn to gold as he picked it up but not nearly so pleased when the meat became hard, cold metal as soon as it touched his mouth. He was hungry. But any food that he touched was transformed instantly into inedible gold.

For a while King Midas hoped that he could avoid the fulfilment of his wish in this one area. He tried all sorts of schemes—having someone pour water into his open mouth or drop a morsel of food into it. Nothing did any good. Anything that he touched, or that touched him, turned into gold.

King Midas seemed doomed to starve to death, unable to eat or drink. Remorse for his greedy desire for gold filled his heart. He began to weep and to pray to the god who had granted his wish to take away the power that had become a curse. At last Bacchus heard him and took pity. The god told Midas that if he washed himself in the nearby river the spell would be revoked.

Midas rushed to the river, plunged in, and the water did wash away his magic power. However, as a consequence, the sands of the river turned to gold.

The river in which he bathed was the Pactolus, the same river that in later years yielded much gold for Croesus, king of Lydia.

Nathaniel Hawthorne's Version

The old legend has been retold many times during the centuries. One well-known version is by Nathaniel Hawthorne, the nineteenth-century American writer who retold many Grecian myths for young people in a book called *Tanglewood Tales.*

In his version of the Midas legend, Hawthorne added another element to the story. As he told it, Midas had a little daughter named Marigold who was dearer to her father than anything on earth—except gold. After Midas discovered that his food and drink turned to gold at his touch, his daughter came in and asked why he seemed so disturbed. He put his arms around her to reassure her—and she turned to gold.

Midas' horror at the consequences of his wish was thus even greater, and his remorse was inspired by unselfish love as well as the desire to save himself. In Hawthorne's story, Midas broke the spell by bathing in the Pactolus River, just as in the legend. Then, by flinging a pitcher full of the river water over his daughter, he brought her back to flesh-and-blood life.

The Phrygian Cap

Another legend about Midas tells that once he was appointed the judge in a musical contest between Pan—the half-goat, half-man god of forests, fields, and shepherds—who played a pipe, and Apollo, the god of sciences and art, who played a harp. Midas declared that Pan was the better musician. In a rage, Apollo wished onto Midas a pair of ass's ears.

Midas tried to hide this disfigurement by always wearing a peaked cap. Since he was king of Phrygia, the cap became known as a Phrygian cap. Through the ages, to say that someone is "wearing a Phrygian cap" has come to mean that the person in question knows little about music and is trying to hide it in an elaborate way.

13
Croesus

"RICH AS CROESUS" is the phrase people use when they want to say that somebody is wealthy beyond imagining, and they have been using these words for
twenty-five hundred years—ever since the days of a king who was indeed
wealthy and who displayed his wealth and boasted of it until it seemed he was
surely the richest man in the world.

His Country and Times

Unlike Midas, Croesus was a real king who lived in the sixth century B.C.,
about two hundred years before the time of Alexander the Great. Nobody is
sure of the exact dates of his birth or death but he came to his throne about
560 B.C. and reigned for about twenty years.

His kingdom was a country in Asia Minor called Lydia. There is no longer
a Lydia on the map, but at that time it was one of a group of kingdoms in
what is now western Turkey.

When Croesus first became king of Lydia after the death of his father, he
had a wonderful monument built to his father's memory. This was so large
and unusual that it at once became one of the marvels of the world.

After that, Croesus set about acquiring the wealth that made him even
more famous. Lydia had many rich mines. Its chief river, the Pactolus,
glittered in the sun from the gold dust its waters carried. Croesus set men to
working the mines as they had never been worked before and then had the
gold, silver, and precious stones brought to his capital city, Sardis. In Sardis,
there were artisans, metalworkers, and jewelers to work the metal and stones
into all sorts of beautiful and useful objects. Croesus' palace grew more and
more splendid.

Now and then Croesus found reasons to go to war against some of the neighboring kingdoms. Victory in these wars brought him still more wealth. He traded with the Greek city-states along the Mediterranean coast and acquired further riches. He had storehouses filled with bars of gold and silver, great chests of diamonds, sapphires, rubies, and other gems.

Croesus welcomed visitors to whom he could show off these treasures, and he was pleased when word about his riches began to spread. Soon people from as far away as Greece came to visit him and went home to use his name as a byword for wealth.

Then Croesus had a visitor who did not show quite the same awe as all the others had.

Croesus and Solon

Solon was a very wise and well-known Greek leader who had brought great reforms to his native city of Athens. When he was elected an official of the city he helped to make its government more democratic and wrote a system of laws for its citizens. Indeed, his fame as a lawmaker was so great that to this day lawmakers of any country (our own United States senators, for instance) are sometimes called "solons." Still, some Athenian noblemen were so displeased by Solon's activities, that Solon finally decided to leave the city and the country for a while.

Croesus was happy to give Solon sanctuary in Sardis and eager to show the famous man his wealth. After greeting Solon, he summoned guides and told them to show Solon all the treasures of his palace and storerooms.

Solon walked quietly beside the guides and looked at everything, the gold and silver statues and bowls, the floors of marble, the hangings of purple silk, the piled-up treasure in the strong rooms. At last he returned to Croesus.

"Well," said Croesus, "tell me, Solon. Who is the happiest man in the world?"

Solon bowed and said, "Your Majesty, it is Tellus of Athens."

Croesus was astonished. He had been sure that Solon would name him, and he had never heard of the man Solon did name. "Who is Tellus?" asked Croesus.

Solon told Croesus that Tellus had been a citizen of a thriving city, the father of healthy, intelligent children, and that he had died gloriously on the field of battle. All this, in Solon's opinion, made him the happiest of men.

Croesus thought about this a moment, then asked, "All right, who is happiest after him?"

But then Solon spoke of two brothers whose devotion to their ailing mother had caused the goddess Juno to grant them her greatest boon, a peaceful death.

Croesus was angry by this time. "And what of me?" he asked. "What of the happiness of the living king who speaks to you now? Am I less than the unknown dead men you praise?"

Solon answered. "Croesus, do not forget the gods. They dispose of men's lives in their own fashion. You have found great prosperity, I agree, and I am glad for you. But do not say that a man is happy until you know the whole of his life—only say that he is favored by fortune."

Croesus was not pleased by these philosophical words. He turned away from his guest and paid no more attention to Solon during his stay in Lydia.

Years passed before Croesus learned what Solon meant.

Croesus and His Sons

Actually, Croesus had a least two reasons not to consider himself wholly happy. He had two sons. One of them had been born deaf and dumb. There was a prophecy that if Croesus tried to have him cured that the day of the son's cure would be one of great misfortune for the father. His second son was sound and handsome, but Croesus had a terrifying dream about him one night and saw the boy killed by a sharp piece of iron. When he awoke, Croesus was still so alarmed by the dream that he took every step possible to prevent his son being hurt by iron. He refused to allow the boy to join the army. He would not let him use or touch a sword, arrow, or javelin.

Then, one day, the boy won his father's permission to go along on a boar hunt. Croesus thought he had made sure that the boy was protected from any injury, but during the course of the hunt an iron-tipped arrow found his son's heart and killed him.

Croesus was plunged into grief, but somehow he still did not think of Solon's words.

Croesus and Cyrus the Great of Persia

The need to protect his kingdom against the advances of a new, young conqueror from the east aroused Croesus from his grief. Cyrus, King of Persia, was sweeping with his armies westward, winning all the lands that had been part of the empire of the Medes. As Cyrus came farther and farther west with his host, all the kings in that area trembled—the king of Babylon and the pharaoh of Egypt as well as Croesus of Lydia. Croesus wanted to gather his forces to resist Cyrus, but he wondered how successful he would be against the Persian host. He wanted reassurance from the gods that he would be victorious in battle as he always had been before.

The oracles were what men consulted in ancient times to get the advice of the gods. These were spirits, or voices, that dwelt in certain trees, caves or springs, tended by priests. Men brought rich offerings to the dwelling place of the oracle, asked the question they wanted answered, and then, sometimes, the oracle answered them. Often, the oracle's reply was phrased mysteriously, like a riddle, and the questioner had to puzzle a long time to unravel its meaning.

Croesus wanted to be sure that he had the best oracle of all to answer his question so he sent messengers to the best-known oracles in Greece, Egypt, and Asia Minor and gave them all a test question to ask. What would Croesus be doing at the very moment that the messenger spoke to the oracle? Croesus then planned to be doing something very odd at that moment. At home, on the day arranged for all the messengers to consult the various oracles, Croesus set himself to boiling the flesh of a turtle and a lamb in a bronze cauldron.

When the messengers returned, two brought replies that showed that the oracles questioned had been able to tell exactly what the king was doing at the crucial moment. Croesus was convinced he had found two very reliable oracles. He sent his messengers back to these two oracles with more lavish gifts to ask what his chances were if he went to war against Cyrus of Persia.

The same reply came back from both oracles. "If he takes up arms, he will destroy a great empire."

Croesus was delighted. He translated this answer to mean that he would destroy the empire of Cyrus. He readied his army and set forth to meet Cyrus and the Persian host.

His Defeat

The two armies clashed, and almost at once the Persians were pushing back the Lydians, finally forcing them to retreat into Sardis and take refuge behind its walls. Cyrus then proceeded to storm the city, and Persian soldiers were soon clambering up and over the walls. Croesus, his deaf-and-dumb son beside him, was fighting as desperately as any foot soldier. Suddenly his son saw a Persian soldier behind his father, raising a javelin to hurl at the king. In his horror, the deaf-and-dumb boy spoke for the first time in his life. "No, no, do not kill Croesus!"

The prediction made about the deaf-and-dumb boy long before had come true. He was cured at the moment of his father's greatest misfortune.

How Croesus Remembered Solon

Sardis was taken by the Persians. Croesus was captured, bound, and led before his conqueror, Cyrus. Cyrus did not hesitate in deciding the fate of the vanquished king. Croesus, along with a group of Lydian nobles, would be burned alive.

Croesus was led up onto the pyre where the wood was piled for the fire. Now, as the soldiers chained him to the stake, he remembered what Solon had said long before. "Do not say any man is happy until you know the whole of his life."

Croesus groaned. Then "Solon, Solon, Solon!" he cried.

Cyrus heard him speak. "What is he saying?" he asked those about him. "Send someone to find out."

An aide hurried to Croesus and asked him what his words had meant. Croesus said, "I was remembering a man whose advice would have been more profitable to me than the greatest wealth."

These words were translated to Cyrus who wanted to hear more.

"Explain yourself," the interpreter said to Croesus as the soldiers began piling sticks and logs about him.

"What does it matter now?" asked Croesus. "Why cannot you leave me alone?" But then, as the soldiers brought more fuel, he began to tell his story. He said he had once believed himself the happiest man on earth because he was so rich. The soldiers touched their torches to the kindling piled around

him, and Croesus told of Solon's visit and Solon's warning that wealth was only a temporary good fortune, and no man could be called happy until the whole course of his life was known.

Flames were shooting up from the wood around Croesus by the time his story had been translated to Cyrus. Suddenly the Persian king was filled with pity for the king whom he had condemned to death.

"Put out the fire!" Cyrus ordered.

The soldiers hurried to try to do his bidding, running for pails of water, snatching away burning pieces of wood. But already the fire was burning so fiercely that these efforts had no effect. The flames leaped higher and higher around Croesus.

The doomed king turned his face toward the sky. "Oh gods of Greece," he cried, "if ever the gifts and offerings I made to you in the past found favor in your sight, remember and save me now."

Suddenly a great black cloud scudded across the sky and covered the sun. There was a clap of thunder and a deluge of rain. In seconds, the rain had put out the fire around Croesus.

The soldiers untied Croesus from the stake and led him to Cyrus. Cyrus spoke kindly and courteously and asked Croesus if he had any requests.

Now that his life was saved, Croesus wanted to know why the oracles had deceived him as to the outcome of his battle with Cyrus. Cyrus agreed to send messengers to the oracles, asking for an explanation.

When the messengers returned they told Croesus what the oracles had replied. They had told him the truth when they said that if he took up arms against Cyrus a great empire would be destroyed. Croesus had interpreted the oracles the way he wanted, deciding they meant Cyrus' empire. They had meant his own.

"My downfall was my own fault," said Croesus quietly.

His misfortunes had made him a much wiser and more thoughtful man than he had been when good fortune favored him. He was, in fact, so wise and thoughtful that Cyrus made him a trusted advisor. Croesus lived in peace and honor in Cyrus' court for the rest of his life. He had learned Solon's lesson well—that riches alone do not make a happy or fortunate man.

14
Ahab

A CERTAIN VINEYARD was what Ahab wanted—that was all. The vineyard was on a sunny slope of ground adjoining the palace grounds and Ahab, king of Israel, saw it and thought what a pleasant site it would be for a herb garden. He found out that the vineyard belonged to an old man named Naboth. Then he went to Naboth and offered him either gold for the vineyard or another better one in exchange.

But Naboth had inherited the land from his father, who had inherited it from his father in turn. The vineyard meant something special to Naboth and he refused to sell it.

Ahab went back to his palace displeased and angry. He lay down on his couch with his face to the wall. His wife, Jezebel, came in, saw him so, and asked what was the matter. Jezebel was beautiful and willful, accustomed all her life to having her own way. She was astonished that Ahab seemed to think that he could not take Naboth's vineyard no matter what Naboth said.

"Are you not king of Israel?" she asked him. But when Ahab still refused to believe that this gave him the right to simply take the vineyard from Naboth, Jezebel laughed.

"Arise, and eat bread, and let thine heart be merry," she said to him. "I will give thee the vineyard of Naboth. . . ."

Ahab got up as she bade him. He went to eat. He did not ask how Jezebel planned to get the vineyard for him. He was content to let her do whatever she wanted, so long as he did not have to take any responsibility for it.

Jezebel's Scheme

Jezebel followed a very simple course. She wrote to all the nobles of the city telling them that Naboth should be put on trial for blasphemy against

God and the king. She asked that Naboth be condemned to death. She sealed the letters with the king's seal.

The nobles acted promptly. They sent men to seize Naboth in his vineyard. He tried to protest, but they dragged him to the center of the city, paying no attention to anything he said. A group of judges was waiting, and a big crowd of people had collected. Two men came forward as witnesses and said that they had heard Naboth blaspheming against God and the king. Naboth denied the charge and said he did not know the witnesses. It did no good. The judges pronounced the sentence. Naboth should be stoned to death. At once guards dragged Naboth to the stoning place, the crowd following. Then everyone in the crowd picked up stones and threw them at Naboth. Stones battered the old man's body and face until at last he fell to the ground, bleeding and broken. And still the crowd threw stones until he was dead.

The news was brought to Jezebel that her wishes had been followed. She went to Ahab and smilingly told him that he had his desire. Naboth was dead and the vineyard was his. Once again Ahab asked no questions. Instead he hurried to the vineyard and began planning the changes he would make.

The Lord's Judgment

In his desire for the vineyard Ahab had ignored more than what his wife was doing. He had forgotten all about a prophet of the Lord named Elijah, who had made himself the voice of Israel's conscience. Jezebel, who wanted only the priests of her own god, Baal, in Israel, had made Ahab send Elijah into exile in the wilderness some time before. But in the wilderness, Elijah saw the Lord in a vision. The Lord told him of Naboth's fate and then commanded Elijah to go to Ahab and pronounce the Lord's judgment on him.

So Elijah came out of the wilderness and found Ahab in Naboth's vineyard. Ahab was astonished to see the prophet. Elijah simply looked at him and said, "Thus saith the Lord: Hast thou killed, and also taken possession?"

Ahab protested that he had killed no one. He knew nothing about any killing. Elijah brushed aside his protests. Ahab had surely known that Jezebel was doing something, and he easily could have guessed it might be murder. Ahab had to bear responsibility with Jezebel. Then Elijah pronounced the Lord's judgment.

"In the place where dogs licked the blood of Naboth shall dogs lick thy blood, even thine. . . . I will bring evil upon thee, and will take away thy posterity." Then Elijah warned that Jezebel also would die in a horrible way.

Ahab fell to his knees. He admitted that he shared responsibility and was guilty as charged. But he begged that the punishment be made less harsh.

Elijah left Ahab while the king was still humbling himself, and for a long time thereafter Ahab was a changed man. He repented so thoroughly that the Lord finally did make his punishment less severe. He was not killed as Naboth had been but slain in battle. Jezebel's punishment was not changed, however. Later, she died a terrible death. And Ahab's sons died also so he had no descendants, just as Elijah had prophesied.

Ahab in History

Ahab lived from about 900 B.C. to about 853 B.C., in the century after Solomon's reign. He was king of northern Israel and the ten Hebrew tribes there that had finally broken away from the united kingdom that David had created. Ahab was a strong king who kept the many tribes of his kingdom under firm control. He also established friendly relations with the Phoenician cities and colonies farther north and south along the Mediterranean coast. Sidon was the oldest and most famous of these Phoenician cities. Jezebel, whom Ahab married, was the daughter of Sidon's king.

Ahab in the Bible

The biblical story about Ahab, which is told in I Kings, Chapters 16–22, does not dwell on his political or military merits but only on his religious failings. According to the Bible, his great mistake was in marrying the Phoenician princess who did not worship Israel's God but the Phoenician gods, chief of which was Baal. She brought an entourage of priests with her when she came to Israel. She had Ahab build her a fine temple for Baal, and she ordered the slaughter or banishment of many of Israel's prophets. That Ahab allowed her to have her own way in all these matters had already angered the Lord against Ahab even before he coveted the vineyard.

Ahab and Jezebel in Literature

Ahab's name has been a symbol for covetousness and wickedness through the centuries. In Herman Melville's novel *Moby Dick,* the captain of the whaling ship, the *Pequod,* who pursues a great white whale through all the oceans of the world, is named Ahab.

Jezebel's name is heard even more often than Ahab's. Hers is symbolic of any bold, daring woman of loose morals. People often speak of a "painted Jezebel," because of a verse in II Kings. A new king, Jehu, had deposed Ahab's son as king of Israel, and he was coming to Jezebel to slay her.

"And when Jehu was come to Jezreel, Jezebel heard of it, and painted her face and attired her head, and looked out of a window."

15
Henry VIII

THE WORLD REMEMBERS a portrait of Henry VIII—a thick, solid, defiant-look-ing man, his clothes rich and jewel-encrusted. The world remembers that he had six wives, two of whom he had beheaded. It is also remembered that he took over control of the church in England from the traditional authorities in Rome because he did not like the rulings of the Roman authorities as they applied to him. The world thinks of him as eating, drinking, shouting, defy-ing the Pope, defying anyone who thwarted him—a greedy king who wanted his own way in everything and almost always got it.

The picture is not an untrue one, it is just incomplete. Henry was not always the greedy king he finally showed himself to be, and he was also intel-ligent, sometimes brilliant, and often brave.

His Country and Times

Henry was born in 1491, the second son of Henry VII and Elizabeth of York. The date of his birth shows that he was a baby when Columbus dis-covered America and still a boy when John Cabot, exploring for England and sponsored by Henry VII, discovered many areas of the New World. But this sudden enlargement of the known world did not play a great part in Henry's life.

As a boy, he had no thought of ever becoming England's king. His older brother, Arthur, would have that responsibility, and Henry was not sorry. He could see that being king of England was not an easy job. His father, who was the Henry Tudor who had defeated Richard III at Bosworth Field to win the crown, had to be constantly on the alert against plots by members of the York family to take the crown away from him again. He also had to be concerned constantly about England's alliances in Europe. Young Henry could see that

concern in action when his brother, Arthur, just fifteen, was married for reasons of state to the equally young Catherine of Aragon, daughter of King Ferdinand and Queen Isabella of Spain.

Meantime, Henry, the second son, not yet the gross, overbearing character that the world remembers, could devote himself to books and sports. He was an excellent scholar, doing especially well in languages, poetry, and music. He was deeply interested in religion. He also loved all sorts of outdoor activity and became an accomplished athlete.

Then, Henry's brother, Arthur, died just a year after his marriage, and Henry was heir to the throne. A few years later, in 1509, Henry VII died, and young Henry became king of England at the age of eighteen.

Very soon after Arthur's death, a plan had been put forward that Henry should marry his brother's young widow. When Henry became king his counselors began insisting on the marriage—for the same reason that Arthur's marriage to her had been made, to strengthen English ties with Spain. Henry had no desire to marry Catherine of Aragon, but finally, against his wishes, he did so.

The Trouble Begins

For a dozen and more years after his marriage in 1509, Henry showed no signs of rebelling against the wife who had been forced on him. He busied himself with war and politics in Europe. For a while, the English were fighting the French in alliance with Spain and Venice. For a while, the warfare was suspended, and Henry and the French king made a show of friendship. They had one meeting in an arena so gorgeously appointed that it was known as the Field of the Cloth of Gold.

Catherine bore Henry children—six in all. But all of them were girls, and all but one, a child named Mary, died in infancy. Finally, this matter of not having a son to be his heir began to disturb Henry, and he started expressing openly his dissatisfaction with a wife who could not bear him a boy-child. He used his small daughter, Mary, as a pawn in his political games in Europe, promising her in marriage to one prince after another, depending on what his relationship to each happened to be. But it was a son that Henry wanted —a son that he needed. Quarreling, plotting, intriguing about who would be the next king of England had led to the long-drawn-out Wars of the Roses in his father's time and before. Plotting and intriguing about the succession had gone on during his father's reign even though Henry VII had two sons. Plotting and intriguing were going on in Henry VIII's time. He had to have a son to make his hold on England secure. And it seemed that Catherine of Aragon could not give him one.

Then Henry fell in love with a young lady of the court named Anne Boleyn. Suddenly, a divorce from Catherine seemed more important to Henry than anything else, and he was on his way to becoming the overbearing man the world remembers.

The Break with the Church

The Catholic Church was traditionally opposed to divorce, and Henry had always been a devout Catholic. He had, in fact, won the title "Defender of the Faith" because he was so strongly against the critics of the Catholic Church in Europe who were breaking from Roman authority and establishing Protestant churches.

For a while, however, Henry thought he could win a special concession from Rome about a divorce because he had been married against his will to his brother's widow—a marriage that had required a special concession from the Pope to begin with. He sent envoys to the Pope in Rome to plead his case. He got opinions from churchmen who agreed with him. He punished or ignored English churchmen who disagreed with him.

Finally, after several years of effort on his part, the Pope gave him the Church's decision—no, he could not have a divorce, nor an annulment of his marriage to Catherine of Aragon.

Henry simply refused to abide by the Pope's decision. Rather than do so, he declared that the Catholic Church in England was no longer under the Pope's authority. He would make himself the Supreme Head of the Church in England. Fortunately for him, most of the members of Parliament were willing to back him up, some because they were sympathetic with the Protestant movement against the Catholic Church and some because they were jealous of the wealth of the Church. Henry pleased all his supporters by confiscating Church property in England and dividing it among them.

He also promptly announced his divorce from Catherine and married Anne Boleyn.

JANE SEYMOUR.

ANNE OF CLEVES.

CATHERINE HOWARD.

CATHERINE PARR.

HENRY VIII.

ANNE BOLEYN.

CATHERINE OF ARRAGON.

His Further Marriages

Soon after Henry and Anne Boleyn were married Anne bore Henry a child—a daughter who was named Elizabeth. Another daughter was disappointing enough, but Henry's infatuation with Anne was already waning. Soon he was in love with a lady named Jane Seymour. Used now to having his own way, Henry arranged to dispose of Anne by having her accused of adultery and then beheaded, a customary form of capital punishment in those days.

Jane Seymour, Henry's third wife, fulfilled his dearest wish by bearing him a son, a boy whom they named Edward. Henry had a male heir to the throne at last. But Jane Seymour died soon after the child was born.

After that Henry was forced into a marriage for reasons of politics to Anne of Cleves. He disliked her and soon arranged for a divorce from her.

His fifth wife was Catherine Howard, who met Anne Bolyen's fate and was beheaded.

His sixth wife, who survived him, was Catherine Parr.

Henry as a Ruler

Henry's many wives and the despotic way in which he took control of the church for his own purposes generally cause people to overlook the fact that, by and large, he was a king who did much more good than harm to England. During his reign England was involved in some warfare, in Europe with France, and, nearer home, with the Scots, who had the French as allies. Two famous English victories over the Scots, the battles of Flodden and Solway Moss, took place during Henry VIII's reign. But actually, England was far less wracked by warfare than it had been in the past or than various countries in Europe were at the same time.

Because Henry took control of the English church at the same time as the Protestants of Europe were breaking with Rome people sometimes think he brought the Reformation to England. But Henry did not make the same kind of changes in church doctrine or ritual as the Protestants in Europe were making. Changes of that nature came slowly as Protestants grew in power in England, and there was very little of the religious persecution that led to so much bloodshed on the continent.

Parliament was strengthened during Henry VIII's reign and the country as a whole grew more prosperous.

Henry's Successors

Henry died in 1547 at the age of fifty-six. Jane Seymour's son, Edward, succeeded him, but was a frail young man and did not live long. Henry's daughter by his first wife, Mary, succeeded Edward. Because she was a devout Catholic and married the equally devout king of Spain, she was encouraged to put the English church back under Roman authority. There was so much persecution of Protestants during her reign that she was called Bloody Mary. After her death, Henry's daughter by Anne Boleyn, Elizabeth, was given the crown and became one of the great queens of history.

PART FOUR

FRIGHTENING KINGS

Ruin seize thee, ruthless king,
  Confusion on thy banners wait. . . .
    The Bard, THOMAS GRAY (1716–1771)

Nero

Attila the Hun

Ivan the Terrible

Richard the Third

16
Nero

"NERO FIDDLES while Rome burns!" people say when someone behaves in a flighty fashion in the face of serious problems. They say it because Nero wasted time on idle amusements when he should have been attending to his empire's needs.

The Real Nero

Nero was an emperor of Rome. He ruled from A.D. 54 to 68, more than a hundred years after Julius Caesar, who did so much to extend Rome's power and who was the last of Rome's rulers under the old republican system. To talk of Nero fiddling while Rome burned is neither fair to him nor accurate. The violin was unknown in his time. Even if it had been invented, it is unlikely that Nero would have been so ridiculous as to play the violin in front of public buildings. He was not always a poor ruler. A wise and faithful tutor counseled him in the early years of his reign and as long as Nero followed his tutor's advice he served his country well. Unfortunately, in later years he came under the influence of bad friends. From then on, he failed to deal properly with one crisis in Rome after another. By the time that he realized he should mend his ways, it was too late.

Nero's Parents

Nero's father was a man called Gnaeus Domitius Ahenobarbus. He died when Nero was three years old. His mother was the sister of the Emperor Gaius Caligula, a tyrant so cruel and ruthless that it is strange his nephew's reputation for wickedness should have eclipsed his. Nero's mother, whose name was Agrippina, was not an especially lovable character either. She was such a schemer that her brother, the emperor, banished her from Rome when Nero was two years old.

Agrippina's ambitions for her son, Nero, were boundless. A throne had been predicted for him, and the prophecy was one that Agrippina believed in with all her heart and soul. When Nero's father died, the boy was moved to the house of an aunt, Domitia. Two slaves, a barber and a dancer, took care of him. They gave him his earliest education. Meanwhile, Agrippina planned and plotted for her return to Rome. When her brother, Caligula, was finally assassinated by an outraged citizen and a new emperor, Claudius, had succeeded him, she won permission to go back to the capital city. For thirteen years thereafter, she did everything she could think of to place Nero on the throne.

Agrippina's Intrigues

To Agrippina's great satisfaction, the wife of Emperor Claudius was publicly disgraced and executed in A.D. 48. Agrippina's next move was to persuade the emperor to marry her. Within a year he did so. He made her his consort in government. But that was not enough for Agrippina. She wanted Claudius to adopt Nero formally. Claudius was so much under her spell that he did so, seeing no danger to himself or to his own son, Britannicus, in strengthening Nero's prospects for the throne.

Seneca, Nero's Tutor

Seneca was a famous Stoic philosopher, writer, and orator of the time, who had been banished from Rome by Claudius. Agrippina, determined to have the best for her son, insisted that Seneca be allowed to return to Rome as a teacher for Nero.

Nero seems to have been a self-willed boy, not an easy child to manage, but under Seneca's influence, the boy learned how to control his behavior. Soon he seemed to be an ideal candidate for the throne.

Of course Claudius' son, Britannicus, also had a good claim to succeed his father. Many Romans thought his claim better than Nero's. Agrippina found out who the supporters of Britannicus were. Then, one by one, she had them banished or done away with.

Those threats taken care of, Agrippina helped to arrange a marriage for Nero with Octavia, daughter of Claudius. It now seemed to her that Nero was only one step from the throne. One person alone remained in his way. That person was Agrippina's husband, the Emperor Cludius.

Claudius' Death

One day when the emperor's trusted freedman was ill and absent from the palace, Agrippina arranged for—or so rumors went—the poisoning of Claudius. On the thirteenth of October, A.D. 54, Claudius died. At once Agrippina insisted that Nero be presented to the soldiers on guard as their new emperor. He was saluted by the troops in the Praetorian camp. In the Senate, he was invested with the honors, titles, and powers of emperor—all on the day of Claudius' death.

Nero's Good Years

In the beginning the new emperor followed Seneca's guidance in almost everything he did. Nero could have assumed the title Father of the Country. Seneca advised him not to. The Romans were pleased that they had a modest ruler. Following Seneca's advice, Nero publicly honored the memory of Claudius and that of his real father, Domitius. This pleased the Roman populace also. He promised to rule according to the maxims of the first emperor of the Roman Empire, the great and popular Augustus. He announced that he would try to avoid the errors that had made Claudius unpopular. And for a time he made good on all his promises.

The people of Rome were delighted. They felt that they had at last a model emperor and that a new era of political freedom had begun. Important questions were discussed freely in the Senate. Taxes were lowered. Abuses were remedied. Nero was so popular with the people that they were not even alarmed when Britannicus, his one-time rival, suddenly died, presumably of poison.

The Bad Influences

Seneca knew that Nero should be shielded from his mother's influence. In

every way he could, the tutor tried to free his former pupil from Agrippina's control. Agrippina did not take competition from Seneca lightly. First she threatened to support the cause of Britannicus. After he was killed, she looked about for a new way to get her son under her thumb. She tried to influence Nero through his wife, Octavia. That was too much even for Nero. He dismissed his mother's guards and placed her in honorable confinement. As long as Agrippina was out of the picture, Nero was free to take the good advice of Seneca. Things went smoothly.

And then another woman entered Nero's life—a wealthy, high-born woman named Poppaea, who fascinated the emperor. Poppaea resented Agrippina even more than Seneca did. She stirred Nero's resentment against his mother until, under Poppaea's influence, Nero plotted his mother's death.

The struggle between the two women discouraged Seneca. He retired from Nero's circle. Without Seneca to advise and guide him, Nero allowed the worst in his nature to come to the surface.

Little by little, the people of Rome began to lose confidence in him.

The End of Octavia

Poppaea and her wealthy friends flattered Nero. His wife, Octavia, was no longer politically useful to him. The more Poppaea fascinated Nero, the more Octavia seemed to be in his way. Poppaea and her friends convinced Nero that Octavia threatened him in some fashion. He banished her to the island of Pandateria, where her life came to a bitter and brutal end.

Disasters Strike Rome

After Octavia's death, Nero married Poppaea. To honor her, her picture was placed on Roman coins, and statues of her were erected in public places. But Poppaea's triumph was short-lived. In the year A.D. 61, the first of a series of disasters struck Rome.

Roman officials in the far-off Roman possession of Britain antagonized their subjects there. Roman legions were rushed to Colchester to put down a revolt. They failed. Soon, what had begun as a small rebellion grew in size. At last the insurgents were put down, and Roman authority was restored in Britain, but none of it had been as easy as the Romans expected.

The uprising in Britain made the people of Rome uneasy. They wondered if their difficulty with Britain might be an omen. Two years later, their fears seemed confirmed. A terrible earthquake shook the Roman city of Pompeii and did much damage. (This was the same city that would be totally buried by an eruption of the volcano Vesuvius sixteen years later.) Another military setback struck the supposedly invincible Roman legions. Troops in Armenia were forced to withdraw.

Then in July A.D. 64 came the fire in Rome, the fire that has continued to blaze around Nero's name throughout the centuries.

The Fire

The Circus Maximus was a building very dear to the Romans—an arena where many of their most exciting sports events were held. On the night of the eighteenth of July, a fire broke out at one end and then quickly spread to destroy the entire building. Then the fire raged on to other parts of the city, leaving a trail of terror, death, and destruction in its wake.

The shocked and terrified Romans felt that the fire had been a punishment and warning from the gods that their city and empire were not being properly ruled. Nero had shown a reckless appetite for luxury and entertainment since Seneca had departed from his life, and so the people felt that somehow he was to blame for what had happened.

Nothing Nero did helped change public opinion. He tried to blame members of an unpopular new religious sect, Christians, for the blaze and had many executed. No one was appeased. Conspiracies against Nero developed. Nero became panic-stricken. He grew suspicious of his friends, and they, in turn, were menaced by his enemies. In the autumn of 65, Poppaea died, leaving Nero more alone than ever. And then, there was a new public disaster. Overcrowding, caused by the fire, led to an outbreak of pestilence that swept through the city.

Nero's End

Nero tried to repair the damage to his reputation. Military expeditions were undertaken to the Caspian Sea and to Ethiopia, but the emperor was no general, and the expeditions failed. He made a good-will tour to Greece, but his self-indulgences annoyed the Greeks and added to his unpopularity at home.

Before long, rebellion had broken out in northern Gaul, in Spain, and along the Rhine. But Nero still had not learned to deal promptly with crisis. He let a week go by before he took any action about the uprising in Gaul, and by then it was too late.

The good things Nero had once done for Rome and the empire were all forgotten now. The Senate turned against him. When the palace guards forsook their positions it was the last straw. Nero left Rome in despair and took shelter in a freedman's villa about four miles out of the city.

He was there when he learned that the Senate had proclaimed another man emperor. He also learned that he had been condemned to death by the Senate. Horsemen were sent to take him to his execution. At their approach, on the ninth of June, A.D. 68, Nero took his own life.

17
Attila the Hun

ATTILA WAS A KING who lived in the middle of the fifth century, when the Roman Empire, to which Julius Caesar had added so many far regions and which was beginning to know trouble in Nero's time, had finally begun to go completely to pieces. The eastern half of the Roman Empire, which included Greece, Asia Minor, the eastern Mediterranean coast, and Egypt, had already broken off from the western half and was ruled by a different emperor (his name was Theodosius in Attila's time). And all over Europe, various Germanic tribes were pushing westward and southward, taking back the land that the Romans had won, chunk by chunk, until soon there would be no western Roman Empire at all.

Attila helped a great deal in this total destruction of the western Roman Empire. He nibbled off some of the eastern Roman Empire too. He was a warrior so feared that men called him the "Scourge of God." He never seemed bothered by his dreadful reputation. In fact, it seemed to aid him in his many wars.

Attila was a Hun. The Huns were a people who lived eastward of the Germanic tribes in Europe, along the steppes of the Volga River. When the Germanic tribes pressed eastward in their direction in the fourth century, the Huns seemed to suddenly explode and spread across Europe, from the far eastern Caspian Sea clear to the Rhine River. For a brief moment in history, the Huns had an empire that extended over a great portion of eastern and western Europe. Attila was the leader of the Huns at the time of their greatest power.

His capital was located close by the site of present-day Budapest. The first eight years of his reign he spent warring against neighboring tribes until one by one he had vanquished them, and his power was supreme in central Europe.

For nearly twenty years he ruled the great Hun empire. Whether he was as cruel as people thought is questionable. Few records were kept in his country in those days, and those that were kept are difficult to verify. All the same, his triumphs in battle are facts of history. So is his unpredictable and often illogical behavior. Attila was an extraordinary king, even in the tumultuous times when he lived.

Attila Becomes King

Attila had a brother whose name was Bleda. They were nephews of King Roua of the Huns. When the king died in A.D. 433, the two nephews shared the throne. Little is known about Bleda except that he died twelve years after ascending the throne with Attila. Because Attila's reputation was so fearsome, many people suspected that he had arranged Bleda's death.

Attila's size was in contrast to his blustering personality. He was short of stature, with a large head, snub nose, and deep-set eyes. His hair turned gray at an early age. His proud step, however, and his haughty manner made it clear that he regarded himself superior to everyone.

Honoria's Ring

In the early days of Attila's reign, he received a curious communication from the Eastern Roman Empire. The emperor of the Eastern Empire, Theodosius, had a granddaughter named Honoria. Honoria fell in love with one of the chamberlains of her grandfather's palace. Her grandfather, who hoped that she would make a brilliant marriage, was much disturbed. To prevent her from running away with the chamberlain, he arranged for her to be carefully guarded.

But Honoria was much too willful to accept her grandfather's plans for her. Secretly, she sent her ring to Attila, king of the Huns, and asked him to be her deliverer and her husband.

It is doubtful that Attila ever considered marrying Honoria. However, he accepted the ring. From then on, whenever it suited his convenience, he proclaimed himself Honoria's betrothed. Honoria gained nothing by sending her ring to Attila, but Attila had an excuse for many wars or threats of wars.

Periodically he would threaten some part of Theodosius' empire and protest that he did it only because Honoria had wronged him in some way. Theodosius, a gentle and peace-loving man, always honored Attila's demands. Perhaps he felt responsible for his granddaughter's foolish and headstrong acts. In any case, so long as he lived, Theodosius paid tribute in goods and gold to Attila whenever he asked for them.

Attila and the Western Roman Empire

Theodosius died in A.D. 450, as the result of a fall from a horse. His throne was taken by a brave and experienced soldier named Marcian. Marcian stood up to Attila as Theodosius had not been willing to do. He ordered all payments of tribute stopped. He answered an insulting message from the Hun fearlessly.

Attila did not take up Marcian's challenge. He seems to have accepted the change in regime philosophically. Instead of declaring war against Marcian, Attila decided to turn his attention to the western half of the Roman Empire. The Roman emperor in the west was Valentinian III.

Attila Challenges all Europe

Valentinian had no responsibility for Honoria's real or fancied misdeeds, but Attila never concerned himself with logic. He demanded from Valentinian one half of his domains as Honoria's dowry. Then he allied himself with the Franks and the Vandals (a warlike people who came from northern Africa and had invaded Spain from there), and led a huge army to the Rhine River.

In the spring of A.D. 451, he crossed the Rhine with his army and began to lay waste to many cities in that part of Europe that we now know as Belgium. From there he marched until he reached the Loire River. There he prepared to lay siege to the city of Orleans.

The people of Orleans made a heroic effort to defend their city but had little chance against Attila. However, Valentinian's Roman forces had allied themselves with some of the fighting Goths of western Europe to create a large army. Attila's scouts saw this army from a distance, marching to the rescue of Orleans. Attila suddenly decided to retreat from Orleans.

Perhaps the Roman-Gothic forces suspected cowardice in Attila. At any

rate, they chased him and his army and pursued them to the city of Troyes. There Attila halted and offered battle.

The fight between the Huns of eastern Europe and the Roman-Gothic forces was one of the most decisive battles of history. It lasted for a day. The number of killed has been estimated as between a hundred and seventy-three thousand and three hundred thousand, but whatever the figure exactly, the slaughter was tremendous. The king of the Visigoths was killed, and as night fell it seemed that Attila would now be able to extend the power of the Hun's empire all the way to the Atlantic Ocean.

The next day, however, with the unpredictability that he always showed, Attila and his forces marched away.

The Challenge to Italy

Until the year 452 none of Attila's enemies seemed ever to have thought of dealing with him in the simplest way of all. They never just asked him to leave them alone. In that year, however, as Attila started to move his armies into Italy, a deputation of Roman Senators, headed by Pope Leo I, met him on the banks of the river Mincio. (Christianity by this time was no longer a despised new religion but had been adopted as the official religion of both the eastern and western Roman Empire. As a result, the Popes, originally bishops of the Church, had increased their power until they were actually more powerful than the emperors.)

Pope Leo and his group knew Attila planned to conquer Italy. They knew he had no particular reason to listen to their arguments. His excuse for the attack was the same old one of his unfulfilled engagement to Honoria. But instead of offering battle and instead of arguing that his excuse for invasion was senseless, the Pope and the senators with him disarmed Attila by simply asking that he spare Rome.

Attila yielded. His sence of humor came to the fore. Jokingly, he said that he knew how to conquer men, "but the lion and wolf are too strong for me." The pope's name, Leo, is the Roman word for lion. The wolf, lupus in the Roman language, was the symbol of Rome.

One Last Surprise

Before he left the banks of the Mincio, Attila told Pope Leo and the senators that he would return unless the wrongs of Honoria were redressed. However, he never made another expedition to Italy. In the following year, he married a girl named Ildico. A great banquet was held to celebrate the marriage. The next night, to everyone's amazement, Attila died. Naturally there were rumors that his death had been caused by violence, but most people believed that he died from natural causes. He was always an intemperate man, and it seemed likely that he had celebrated his marriage to Ildico with more food and drink than were good for him.

Attila's Legend

Because he controlled so much of central Europe and because he inspired so much fear everywhere, stories about Attila, the Scourge of God, were told in many lands. German-speaking people call him Etzel in the tales they tell about him. To Scandinavians, he is known as Atli.

The City of Venice, Souvenir of Attila

Very soon after Attila's death the vast empire he had ruled over began to crumble. It had been divided among his many sons, and when the Germanic tribes began to revolt against Hun rule, the sons of the Scourge of God were unable to fight back successfully. Soon the Huns had retreated far back into eastern Europe.

Some Huns, however, remained in western Europe. There were, especially, many fugitives from Attila's march on northern Italy. They sought shelter around the lagoons along the northern shore of the Adriatic Sea. There they laid the foundations of Venice. If no other good came out of Attila's military might, Venice, the beautiful city of palaces and canals, owes its existence to the fearsome, unpredictable Hun.

18

Ivan the Terrible

IVAN IV WAS A king of Russia, its first ruler to be called a tsar. He accomplished much that was good in his lifetime, but some of his deeds were truly fearsome. As a result, his enemies called him Ivan the Terrible. Then, when he was fifty, he grew angry with his son one day and struck the boy in his rage. The blow proved fatal. Ivan could not forgive himself for he had loved his son dearly. He too began to think of himself as Ivan the Terrible, and he is remembered by that name to this day.

Ivan's Childhood

Ivan was born in 1530, the son of Vasily III Ivanovich, who was called the Grand Duke of Muscovy although he was actually the ruler of Russia. It was a time when all sorts of new ideas were exciting and troubling the people of western Europe. The new world of America had been discovered; new ideas about religion were being either embraced or fought over. None of these new ideas and discoveries was causing any stir in Russia, however, for it was a country that seemed remote from Europe both geographically and emotionally, backward and primitive in its ways.

Ivan's father died when he was three, and the child was proclaimed grand duke of Muscovy in his stead. Then his mother, Elena Glinska, died when he was eight. This left the boy to be raised by the noblemen attached to the court. Russian noblemen were called boyars, and boyars in general were a cruel and conniving lot. They cared little about human dignity or human life but were interested only in their own power and importance.

The boyars who raised Ivan hoped to use him for their own ends. They taught him to be brutal, but his conscience was stronger than they knew. He yearned for kindness and affection. He took to reading the scriptures and old chronicles of the Slavonic people. This reading comforted him and also convinced him of his own divine authority.

In 1546, when he was sixteen, he took control of the government and the following January was crowned tsar of Russia. As soon as he had this supreme authority, he treated the boyars savagely. His hatred for them never faded and influenced his actions for the rest of his life.

Ivan as Tsar

After Ivan had destroyed the boyars' hold on the government, he made a sincere effort to overcome Russia's backwardness. He chose intelligent, progressive men as advisors. And he summoned a national assembly—the first national assembly his country had ever known. He made a public confession of his youthful sins and promised the assembly that Russia would be governed justly and mercifully throughout his reign. He asked religious leaders for suggestions on improving the government.

Then Ivan backed up his promises with deeds, and for ten years and more he gave Russia exceptionally good government. He extended Russian power, and with it, Christianity, into Asia and brought the Finnick and Tartar tribes under his rule.

Ivan's Difficulties

Ivan's good intentions pleased the Russian people, but the rulers of western Europe made it difficult for him to accomplish much that he wished. They preferred Russia to be a backward neighbor, and whenever possible they hindered Ivan's plans. Ivan realized Russia's need for more industry and wanted to train his people for such work by bringing skilled workers and artisans to Russia from other countries. The powerful emperor of the Holy Roman Empire, Charles V, ruined his hopes for this by refusing workers permission to migrate to Russia. Ivan realized that he would have to fight to gain his ends. However, he was not very successful in the battles he undertook to try to win a Baltic seaport for Russia.

His counselors then began advising him to attack the Crimea, a rich region to the South, on the shore of the Black Sea. It was a territory which had been held for years by the Turks. Ivan did not want to attack such powerful enemies as they were and also felt that a move against the Crimea would stretch his supply lines too far. Still his advisors would not stop talking about the Crimea and Ivan became convinced their counsel was not to be relied on.

Then Ivan became gravely ill, and as he lay at the point of death he realized that the men around him were denying the claims of his infant son to succeed him if he should die. When Ivan recovered, the streaks of harshness in his nature were deeper and stronger than they had ever been before. He became tyrannical. And still more troubles rained upon him. His wife died. One of his sons died. And at about the same time, his closest friend, Prince Kurbsky, deserted him. Ivan seemed to lose all faith in God and man. He began treating government officials brutally. The whole atmosphere around him began to be charged with fear and suspicion.

Finally, in 1564, Ivan seemed to realize what he was doing to his people and himself. He announced his intention to abdicate. But the common people, whom he had always favored, implored him to come back. They made it clear that they wanted him as their ruler and no one else.

The Oprichnina

Ivan at last agreed to continue as tsar on condition that he might set up a special corps of men to fight treason. This special corps, called the *Oprichnina,* was made up of six thousand carefully selected boyars and lower dignitaries. These men, responsible to no one but Ivan, soon had begun a reign of terror in Russia. They played upon the harsh and gloomy tsar's suspicions and urged him on to order acts of unprecedented cruelty. Under their influence, Ivan had a high church dignitary of Moscow killed, and, listening to their tales of conspiracy, he had all the inhabitants of the city of Novgorod massacred.

The Tragic Blow

Fits of repentance followed most of Ivan's cruelest acts. Then, after these, there were sometimes brief interludes of something like peace. He was always trying again, trying to behave quietly and generously, trying to find some kind of serenity. Like Henry VIII of England, he repeatedly sought happiness in marriage. (Henry was still reigning in England when Ivan was a boy.) Ivan even outdid Henry by marrying seven times, but cruel as he was his unwanted wives were not killed as Henry's were. Ivan merely encouraged the discarded wife to enter a nunnery.

During the 1570's, Ivan engaged in one small war after another. He lost all of them but one. His single success brought the kingdom of Serbia under his control.

And then, in 1580, overmastered by another of his transports of senseless rage, he struck his son Ivan the blow that killed him.

The Final Remorse

This time, Ivan's remorse for his own action was boundless. Grief-stricken and full of self-loathing, he felt himself unworthy of the throne and tried again to abdicate as tsar.

Once again he was refused any comfort. His old enemies, the boyars, were so suspicious of him that they could not accept anything he said at face value. Fearing trickery, they refused to obey any ruler but Ivan himself. And so the bereaved father was unable to make the one gesture that might have made his grief more bearable.

Three years later, on the eighteenth of March, 1584, Ivan suddenly fell backward in his chair while playing chess. He seemed to know that death was near. He asked to join a strict religious order of hermits. He took the name of Jonah, after the biblical character whose faint-heartedness in following the commands of God caused him to be cast into the sea. And so, when he died later in 1584 he was no longer Ivan the Terrible, at least not in his own mind, but the suffering Jonah who learned at last that God's will could not be denied.

Ivan the Good

In spite of the fear and terror Ivan often brought to his people, he had brought some blessings to Russia. Because of his own hatred of the boyars, he had broken their hold on the government and established the authority of the tsar.

He was a man of intelligence and learning, and he was responsible for introducing printing (which had been invented a century earlier in Ger-

many) into Russia. He very much admired the English and looked to England for friendship, hoping that Russia might finally share in the benefits of England's flowering civilization. At one point, while he was still married to his fifth wife, he thought of marrying one of the ladies of Queen Elizabeth's court.

Boris Godunov

Still more shadows of cruelty and harshness fall on Ivan's memory with the name of Boris Godunov. Godunov was a favorite of Ivan's. Godunov's sister married Ivan's son and heir, Feodor, and after Ivan's death, when Feodor became tsar, Boris Godunov practically ruled Russia, as a regent. When Feodor's younger brother was killed, most people thought Godunov was responsible. Godunov ruled strongly and not unwisely while he held power but finally lost popular support.

Boris Godunov's dramatic career was the subject of a drama by the Russian playwright Alexsandr Pushkin. This drama in turn inspired an opera by another Russian, Modest Moussorgsky.

19

Richard the Third

FEW ENGLISH KINGS have a worse reputation than Richard III. Most people think he was sly, ambitious, and murderous to an almost inhuman degree. Above all, the world remembers him with horror because of the terrible fate that befell his two young nephews. The boys were slain in their sleep one night in the Tower of London. Their death was discovered shortly after Richard deprived the older boy of the throne.

The Mystery of Richard III

Whether Richard was responsible for the boys' death—whether he was in any way the monster most people think that he was, is a mystery. There is no doubt that he was ruthless and ambitious and responsible for some political murders. But the most damaging stories about him were told by those who followed him to power and were not generally circulated until long after Richard's death. It was to the advantage of the new rulers to paint Richard as a complete villain so the stories grew more and more exaggerated.

One story claimed that he was born not only misshapen but with streaming hair and a full set of teeth. Some reports said that he was hunchbacked, others that he had a withered arm and that later, when he was grown, he accused two ladies of the court of inflicting this infirmity on him through sorcery.

Finally, a hundred years after Richard's death, William Shakespeare used the folklore about him when he made him the subject of one of his historical plays. *The Tragedy of Richard III*. The Richard that Shakespeare depicted is the one that is remembered today. His shadow quite blots out any redeeming qualities that may have existed in the real Richard III. Shakespeare's Richard is a hunchback who calls himself "deform'd, unfinish'd," and at the very start of the play he announces his evil plans.

RICARDVS · III · ANG · REX

"I am determined to prove a villian
And hate the idle pleasures of these days.
Plots have I laid, inductions dangerous. . . ."

Through the course of the play his various plots are put into action, there
are revelations of one murder after another that he has committed, until at
last he is killed in battle by a rival claimant to the throne, with everyone
relieved to have him out of the way.

Richard's Times

Richard was born in 1452 and lived in violent times when plotting, bloodshed, and warfare constantly involved most of the English nobility and sol-
diering classes. The Hundred Years War with France was just over when he
was born, but the English, instead of settling back to an interlude of peace,
embarked at once on a series of wars among themselves over who was to be the
English king.

These wars were romantically called the Wars of the Roses, but their name
was the only romantic thing about them. Two royal houses, or families—the
House of York, which had the white rose as its symbol, and the House of
Lancaster, which had a red rose emblem—each maintained that one of its
members was the rightful king. Battle followed battle as first one group then
another won a victory. Depending on which side won, Yorkists went into
exile and Lancastrians held power, or Yorkists held power and Lancastrians
went into hiding to plot their next move.

Richard's Childhood

Richard was involved in this tumult from his earliest days for he was the
youngest son of the Duke of York, who claimed the crown under the white
rose banner. Parliament accepted the duke as king, but he never reigned. He
was killed in a battle with the Lancastrians when Richard was eight. In spite
of that Yorkist defeat, Richard's older brother, Edward, managed to have
himself chosen king a few months later. Edward was aided in this by relatives
on his mother's side. She was Cicely Neville, a member of one of the most
prominent families in England. A nephew of hers, the Earl of Warwick,
known as "the kingmaker," was Edward's chief ally.

The young Richard, who had been sickly since birth and whose nervous temperament was not helped by all the warfare around him, was fond of his handsome, energetic older brother. And the new king, Edward IV, returned the affection. He soon named his young brother Richard the Duke of Gloucester, gave him great tracts of land, and appointed him, young as he was, admiral of the fleet.

But no real peace came to England with Edward IV's ascension to the throne. The Lancastrians rallied and finally forced Edward to flee to Holland while they put their own king, Henry VI, back on the throne.

Richard, loyal to his brother, went with him to Holland as a matter of course. He was eighteen by this time, old enough to bear a full share in any fighting or plans for fighting. And when, a year later, Edward IV sailed back to England to challenge the Lancastrians again, Richard did his part in helping to bring about a Yorkist victory at the famous battle of Tewkesbury. Directly after this battle, the oldest son of the Lancastrian king was killed and several days later Henry VI himself died in the Tower of London. Shakespeare—and legend—both claim that Richard was responsible for these two deaths. However they came about, with the Lancastrian king and his heir both dead, there were no immediate Lancastrian contenders for the crown and Edward IV could settle down as the undisputed ruler of England for a while.

Troubled Years

Still violence and rumors of violence continued to surround Richard, Duke of Gloucester. He quarreled bitterly with another of his brothers, the Duke of Clarence. When Clarence died it was the popular belief that Richard was responsible.

But Richard continued to serve his oldest brother, Edward IV, as an able military commander, and he fought a victorious campaign against the Scottish lords who constantly harassed their English neighbors during these years.

Then, in 1483, Edward IV died. He left two sons, Edward and Richard. The thirteen-year-old Edward was the obvious heir to the crown, but since he was too young to rule, his dying father had appointed the boy's uncle, Richard, as his guardian. He had also named Richard Protector of the Kingdom until the boy should come of age.

The Crown as a Prize

Not everyone was pleased by the naming of Richard as regent.

The family of the dead king's wife—the Woodvilles—wanted to direct the regency themselves. Enemies of the Woodvilles urged Richard to thwart them by assuming the crown himself. They found a pretext for declaring that the dead king's marriage to Elizabeth Woodville had not been legal so as to cast doubt upon young Edward's right to succeed his father.

Finally, a group of noblemen met and declared that Edward IV's marriage had been invalid. They then offered Richard the crown. Richard made some slight protest that he did not want to reign and then quickly accepted the offer. He was crowned king of England the next day, to rule as Richard III.

The Nephews in the Tower

As soon as the questions about their father's marriage had arisen, Richard had arranged that his young nephews, Edward and Richard, be taken into custody and lodged in the Tower of London. Whether they were flung into a cell and cruelly mistreated, as legend claims, or whether they were treated well and allowed to play within the walls, as one or two reports of the time seem to indicate, no one knows for sure.

However, soon after their uncle took over the throne, a movement was organized to release the boys. Then it became known that the little princes were dead.

Who had been responsible for their deaths no one knew. It might have been one of Richard's supporters who feared that Richard's claim to the crown would never be safe while the boys lived. It might have been Richard himself. But the story that tells in great detail of two men coming and smothering the boys in their bedclothes one night and then burying them at the foot of a staircase in the tower was not told until twenty-five years later.

Richard III as King

Richard III faced a revolt among some of his subjects soon after becoming king. He managed to put it down and had the leader of the revolt executed. Then it seemed that he tried very hard to show himself a just and generous ruler. But rumors about the fate of his nephews made many people suspicious of him, and he had less than two years to try to change the general opinion that he was a cruel and ruthless man.

By the summer of 1485, another claimant to the crown from the Lancastrian line had appeared. He was Henry Tudor, Earl of Richmond. who was related, far, far back, to Henry V. Because he also had Welsh ancestry, the people of Wales, generally hostile to both Yorkists and Lancastrians, rallied to his banner, to swell the ranks of the Lancastrians already there.

Henry Tudor (also called Richmond) marched eastward from Wales into England with his forces. Word of his coming reached Richard III, and he hastened to gather together his army and march out to meet his challenger. Many men on whom he had been counting for support refused to fight for him. Richard muttered "treason," and grimly went on with his preparations to repulse Henry Tudor.

Bosworth Field

Richard III and Henry Tudor and their opposing armies met at Bosworth Field, almost in the center of England, in August, 1485. There was a fierce and bloody battle, and finally Richard's horse was shot from under him.

"A horse, a horse, my kingdom for a horse!" are the famous words that Shakespeare had Richard cry at this fearful moment.

Another horse was hurried to him but all of Henry Tudor's forces were sweeping down on him. Soon a dozen men surrounded Richard and were hacking their swords and broadaxes through his armor, beating him lifeless to the ground.

So Richard III lost his life, and England had a new ruler.

Henry VII, Richard's Successor

Henry Tudor, Earl of Richmond, was immediately acknowledged the new king by Parliament. As Henry VII, he founded a new line of English kings— the Tudor dynasty. In many ways he justified the hopes of the English noblemen who had defected from Richard III to support him. He ended the exhausting struggle between the Yorkists and Lancastrians and united the

white rose and the red by marrying one of the daughters of Edward IV.

During his reign, peace came at last to England. The country's ruined finances were brought back into order and crops could grow again on a countryside no longer criss-crossed by armies.

During the reigns of his descendants, Henry VIII and Queen Elizabeth I, England's fortunes further improved and the nation moved to a new greatness in many areas, such as exploration, trade, and literature.

By that time, Richard III had begun to seem the black villain the world remembers—thanks to Tudor historians who wanted no more trouble from die-hard Yorkists. The Tudor historians were the ones who told the story of the little princes, murdered in the tower. They were the ones who described Richard as a hunchback.

But still it was a Tudor historian who granted Richard III courage as well as ruthlessness and wrote that he "was killed fighting manfully in the thickest press of his enemies."

PART FIVE

WISE AND THOUGHTFUL KINGS

He thinks like a philosopher and acts like a king. . . .
Confessions, JEAN-JACQUES ROUSSEAU (1712–1778)

Hammurabi

Ikhnaton

Solomon

20
Hammurabi

In order that "the strong should not oppress the weak, and that widows and orphans should be rightly dealt with," Hammurabi had a pillar of stone inscribed with two hundred and eighty-two legal precepts. The stone, eight feet in height, was prominently placed in the city of Babylon so that all who lived or visited there could have no excuse for not knowing the laws of the land.

King Hammurabi, who gave the world its first great code of laws, lived some two thousand years before Christ and several centuries before the Israelites received the Ten Commandments from Moses. Some scholars say he lived about 2100 B.C. Others, following another system of dating, say that he lived about 1700 B.C. Whichever system is followed, he was one of the earliest kings to rise above the anonymous groups of primitive men and show himself as a trail blazer on the road to civilization. (King Minos of Crete, whose story can also be found in this book, probably lived about the same time. Ikhnaton of Egypt, whose story is also told, lived several hundred years later.)

His Country and Times

Hammurabi lived and fought and ruled in Babylonia, an ancient country located in the region now called Iraq. Babylonia was the land that knew the great flood of which the Bible tells. It was the land where, long before the flood, perhaps as far back as 5000 B.C., the world's first cities were built.

The Great Invention

The gifts of nature were one reason for this early civilization. The sun gave Babylonia three growing seasons annually. Two great rivers, the Tigris and the Euphrates, continually replenished the fertility of its soil with waters rich in organic matter drained from mountainsides thousands of miles away.

Olive trees flourished, and livestock grazed upon the sunny slopes and plateaus of the north. In the south, wheat, barley, sesame, apples, dates, and many kinds of shelled fruits grew wild along the marshes. Fish were plentiful in the rivers, and game ran along the shores.

All these riches of nature inspired the early inhabitants of this area to one of the great agricultural inventions of all time—the invention that made cities possible. Canals were the invention: a system of channeling water, damming it and then releasing it, so that the heavy rains of one season could be used to water the crops of another season when rains were scarcer, and so that dry lands with no rivers could be watered at will.

Once men had invented this wonderful idea, other things followed. Men learned that instead of each man raising food for his own family a few workers could raise food for many. Some workers could devote themselves to building and working the canals, some to storing and distributing the food that was grown, some to building shelters to store the food, or constructing other public buildings. With differentiation of labor, the first cities came into being.

The Ziggurat, Temple of Ancient Babylonia

The chief public building in every city in these ancient times was an impressive tower called a *ziggurat*. This was a pyramidlike structure of several stories, each story being a square box shape a little smaller than the one beneath it, so that the whole building rose upward with a zigzag profile.

Ziggurats were usually temples to the gods who men believed controlled the weather and the growth and death of living things.

Sargon's Empire

Canals and cities with their ziggurats had come into being long before Hammurabi's time. In fact, this king whom we look back on as living at almost the beginning of time could look back himself at centuries of progress before he was born. Six hundred years before Hammurabi, a conqueror named Sargon had brought Babylonia's mountainous north and southern plain into a single empire, then marched his armies west until his rule extended all the way to Asia's Mediterranean shores. Sargon's was the first great empire in Babylonia's history, and, though it lasted only a little longer than a century, its fame lived on.

Hammurabi's Land

The great Babylonian empire of Sargon's day had shrunk to little more than the city-state of Babylon by Hammurabi's time. When he took over the throne from his father, Sumu-Abi, at the age of twenty-five, there were those who hoped that he would win back some of the ancient kingdom from the enemies who surrounded Babylon. A people called the Elamites controlled the fertile valleys to the south, and many Babylonians wanted Hammurabi to march on the Elamites first of all.

But Hammurabi though young was not reckless. It seemed to him that Babylon had problems that needed solving first. So for six years, Hammurabi devoted himself to restoring law and religion to his city. Then he began forming alliances with other leaders of Semitic peoples, like his own, and at last he embarked on warfare against the Elamites.

For thirty years and more, Hammurabi and his armies were engaged in battle, one place or another. At last the Elamites were conquered, and then Hammurabi made his power felt in Syria and other Mediterranean lands. Finally, thanks to him, Babylonians were reveling in independence, unity, and power. If Hammurabi's empire was not quite as large as Sargon's had been, few of his subjects minded. Hammurabi offered something his people valued even more: wisdom. He was "the lawgiver." His love of justice reinforced his victories.

Wonders of the Babylonian World

In Hammurabi's time, men in the rest of the world were still communicating by grunt and groan, still seeking food with clubs and finding shelter in caves. But in the Tigris-Euphrates valley, the invention of irrigation canals had been only the beginning. Men there spoke a complex and logically constructed language. They had devised cuneiform writing, a simple and practical system for putting down facts and ideas in picture form. They invented the wagon wheel, the plow, and the sailboat. They used calendars, levers, pulleys, measuring instruments, surveying tools, and even the potter's wheel. They designed their ziggurats and other buildings according to sound architectural principles.

Poets, sculptors, and musicians were encouraged in this civilization, and for musical instruments, they had developed harps, lyres, flutes, drums, and tambourines. Artisans worked in gold, copper, bronze, lead, glass, and enamels.

They had a science of medicine, and they manufactured drugs. And, as might be expected of a people who had studied nature well enough to harness water for irrigation, they were interested in all natural phenomena. Astronomers and astrologers mapped out the positions of the stars, and farmers learned how to pollinate plants and trees by hand.

The Story of Gilgamesh, Babylon's Epic

Like most people who attain any kind of civilization, the Babylonians had mythical heroes. One of the chief of these was a hero named Gilgamesh, and an epic was written about him and engraved on twelve stone tablets.

Gilgamesh was a mighty man, and at first he had as a rival a magical creature, half bull, half man, who was known as Engidu. Then Engidu fell in love with a human maiden, compassion was born in him, and he and Gilgamesh became friends. The story continues with an account of the adventures of Gilgamesh and Engidu as they wander the world together looking for the key to immortality.

The End of Hammurabi's Empire

Jealous nomadic neighbors began their attacks on Hammurabi's land soon after his death. They were eager for the rich countryside as pasture land for their cattle and sheep. Finally, they managed to take the country over, and with their coming the rich fruits of civilization were allowed to wither and rot away. The canals clogged up. No one dredged them, and gradually the land lost its fertility.

Centuries later, however, Babylonia knew new periods of glory, first as part of the Assyrian Empire, and then, independently, as the Chaldean, or New

Babylonian Empire. Nebuchadnezzar was the most famous king of this period. Later still, Alexander the Great made Babylon one of his capitals, and it was there that he died.

And then, gradually, Babylonia's glories faded again. Its riches were covered with sand.

Legends about Hammurabi and the code of laws he had devised survived. But the world might still be wondering if King Hammurabi really set forth the early concepts of justice from which our modern law derives if a visitor to Iraq had not grown curious about a mound of sand.

His curiosity led to the discovery, about a hundred years ago, of many Babylonian relics. Among the records and other exciting remnants of the past that were uncovered was a great stone pillar, covered with inscriptions. The pillar was ultimately sent to France, scholars there pored over the inscriptions, and now visitors to the Louvre museum in Paris may see it on display. It is the pillar that stood in the center of Babylon more than four thousand years ago, and inscribed on it is Hammurabi's code of laws.

21

Ikhnaton

A KING NAMED IKHNATON was the first ruler in history to proclaim his belief in a universe created by one god. He was a Pharaoh of Egypt fourteen hundred years before the birth of Christ, a century and more before the Israelite leader Moses received the Ten Commandments from the God of the Israelites. Ikhnaton's god was Aton. Ikhnaton was only fourteen or fifteen years old when he was seized with the belief that shaped his life and insured his fame.

Ikhnaton's Country and Times

Long before Ikhnaton was born, about 1385 B.C., his ancestors had extended Egypt's power into Asia Minor and beyond. The countries they vanquished were rich in jewels and woods and other treasures that Egypt lacked. From Syria south to Canaan, from as far away as present-day Iran, these countries kept the Pharaohs' treasuries filled with precious gifts, with tax monies, and trade revenue.

Egypt itself was rich in gold and grain. And also in labor. For years, captives from defeated armies or descendants of those captives had been kept as slaves to do all the hard or unpleasant tasks. This meant that the Egyptians themselves had easy and agreeable lives.

Ikhnaton was raised in the court of his father, Amenhotep III. It was a happy place, with many physical comforts, and intellectual companionship was always at hand.

Ikhnaton's Name

When Ikhnaton was born, his parents named him Amenhotep after his father and other distinguished members of the dynasty to which he belonged.

Amenhotep means "beloved of Amen." Amen was a sun god, one of many gods Egyptians worshiped.

In 1369 B.C., shortly after Ikhnaton was crowned full regent of his country, he told his people about his devotion to Aton, the one god he believed to be the source of all life. At that time he changed his own name to Ikhnaton. Ikhnaton means "it is well with Aton." Like Amen, Aton was a sun god, but a god who characterized a different aspect of the sun.

Egyptian Beliefs in Ikhnaton's Time

Ikhnaton's proclamation about there being only one god came as a fearful shock to his people. To get any idea of how dismayed they were, one must realize how many different gods they were accustomed to worship.

Almost every aspect of life that they did not understand they assumed was under the control of some special god. And all of the special physical aspects of their country inspired their own particular and unique deities.

The Nile, the chief river of Egypt, determined the food supply of the land. Each year, on or about the twenty-first of June, the Nile rose to overflowing. Then its waters turned a broad strip of desert into marvelously fertile land. At Aswan (where a great hydro-electric dam is now under construction), there is the first of a series of waterfalls that prevented the ancient Egyptians from tracing the river to its source. They had no way of knowing that rains, falling in far-off equatorial Africa, caused the annual flooding. So they worshiped the river as a god.

The surrounding desert also influenced Egyptian religious beliefs and encouraged Egyptians to believe in life after death. The dry desert air acted as a preservative on dead bodies. As a result, Egyptians believed that death merely meant that the spirit had departed from the body for a while and might return at any chosen time. To keep a body safe from harm until the spirit's return, people spent much time and effort on building proper tombs. Pharaohs and nobles had splendid pyramids built for them, and even less wealthy people filled the tombs of loved ones with food, utensils, furniture, everything that a reanimated body would need when its spirit returned.

The bright Egyptian sun was another factor in Egyptian religion. Throughout the day, an Egyptian could count on the companionship of his shadow, but at nightfall it slipped away. To the ancients, the shadow seemed like one's spirit. They imagined death as a long nightfall during which the spirit was away.

The sun's journey across the sky also impressed the Egyptians. They watched the sun rise in the east each morning. When it sank in the west each evening, they assumed it returned to the east through an underground passage. Perhaps on its way back it visited the god who pushed crops from the ground.

The Scarab and the Serpent

Among the kinds of beetle that lived in Egypt was the scarab. The scarab rolls dung into a ball, then pushes the ball into a cavity in the earth. After laying its eggs in the dung ball, the beetle covers the cavity with sand and proceeds to roll another ball into which it lays more eggs. When the eggs are hatched, the young emerging beetles appear to have been self-created. The Egyptians wondered who but a god would have the power to recreate himself, and so, in Egypt, the scarab came to be thought of as sacred.

The snake, too, was considered a supernatural creature in ancient Egypt. Because the larger animals of the region—the hippopotamus, crocodile, boar, lion, and wild cat—stayed clear of populated regions, the snake was about the most dangerous creature the Egyptians knew. Anybody who was able to cure snake bite was assumed to have magical power. Gradually, anybody with the magical power to cure snake bite came to be considered a magician who could help to solve almost any sort of problem in a supernatural way.

Ikhnaton's Philosophy

Hearing about all these various gods, and many more, as he grew up, Ikhnaton began to question the good sense of such beliefs. He was troubled by a popular belief that the sun raced across the sky all day because it was pursued by an enemy. Why, he wondered, should gods be in conflict with each other? Neither could he bring himself to believe in gods who were self-created.

If they exist at all, he reasoned, they must have been created by a force more powerful than themselves.

Finally, he came to his unique conclusion—there was only one supreme source of life. Uplifted and inspired by this vision, he ordered his people to worship only that one supreme god, and he urged them to forsake all their myriad superstitions and try to see life as it really was.

"What is, is good," he said, and he encouraged artists and writers to depict life as it was.

To the dismay of the residents of the capital city, Thebes, he ordered a new capital built for Egypt. But in spite of their protests a handsome new city called Akhetaton rose according to his plans.

Living with Truth

Pharaohs before Ikhnaton had always regarded any public display of emotion as beneath the dignity of royalty. Ikhnaton and his wife, Queen Nefretiti, were proud parents. Although it shocked their countrymen, they refused to hide their affection for their children. Their portraits and statues showed them kissing the children. In these and other ways they sought to demonstrate the value of truth. "Living with Truth" was the name they gave to their plan for emancipating Egypt from the bonds of fear and superstition.

Reactions to the One-God Idea

Some artists and intellectuals accepted Ikhnaton's religious reforms, but most Egyptians were shocked and horrified by them. They thought it better and far, far safer to worship as their ancestors had, for generations past. Wherever they looked, they saw life's blessings. Surely these had been granted by the gods whom they had learned about as children.

Above all, the rich, highly organized and powerful priesthood was angry at Ikhnaton's new idea. Not only was the idea of one god heresy to the priests, it was an idea that was bound to curtail their income and rob them of importance in Egyptian life.

Ikhnaton's Failure

So long as Egypt remained powerful and prosperous, however, the people in general were willing to tolerate their ruler's religious ideas. But unlike his ancestors, Ikhnaton was not a warlike man. When rulers of conquered countries began to plot against him, he relied on the goodness of man to prevail.

Soon the Amorites and Hittites wrested control of Syria from Egypt. The Canaanites and Habiru, forebears of the Israelites, rebelled against Egyptian rule. As Egypt's power waned, reaction to the worship of one god grew.

Ikhnaton died in 1358 B.C. Ikhnaton's heirs could not stem the rising discontent. In a few years the dynasty of which he had been a member came to an end.

A new dynasty was established, and Egypt's new rulers quickly returned to the earlier forms of worship. Every effort was made to banish Ikhnaton from history. The city of Akhetaton was razed. Statues and paintings of Ikhnaton and Nefretiti were destroyed. Their names were removed from public monuments and buildings.

Six hundred years would pass before the world would be ready again to think about the possibility of a single divine power.

Ikhnaton's Reappearance in History

Perhaps because the Egyptians were a nation of record keepers, a number of letters sent to Ikhnaton by heads of vassal states were preserved. In the last century, scholars and archaeologists began to discover and study these letters. From them, they were able to recreate at least an outline of the sort of man Ikhnaton must have been.

In 1912, an archaeologist came upon a limestone and plaster bust of Nefretiti. It was one of the few statues or portraits of the queen that had not been destroyed. The dignity, poise, and beauty of the sculptured queen captured the attention of the world. Reproductions of the bust are made today, and the face of Nefretiti is a familiar sight in many modern homes.

22

Solomon

"Wise as Solomon" is a phrase everybody knows. And almost everybody knows the story of how he settled a quarrel between two mothers in a way that showed an unerring understanding of the human heart. One baby was claimed by both mothers, and there seemed no way to prove which mother was telling the truth about what had happened to lead to such a situation.

Both mothers, who lived in the same dwelling, had had babies at the same time. One night one of the babies died. The difficulty arose because the mother who woke to find a dead baby beside her insisted that the dead child was not hers. She claimed that it was the other woman's child who had died, and that the other woman had exchanged the dead child for her living one while she slept. The other woman, of course, insisted that she had done nothing of the kind and said that the first mother was crazed by grief at having lost her own child. And both fought for possession of the living baby.

Solomon's judges were baffled by the case. They could think of no test to prove which woman had borne the child. Then Solomon said, "Bring me a sword."

The captain of his guards stepped forward and drew his sword. Then Solomon said, "Divide the living child in two and give half to the one and half to the other."

At this, one woman nodded, accepting the decision as fair. The other woman, however, cried out in horror at the thought of the child being killed. "Oh, my lord," she said, "give her the living child and in no wise slay it."

Then Solomon said, "Give her the living child. She is the mother thereof." By his test, the true mother, who would rather give up the child than have it harmed, had been revealed.

The news of this judgment spread through all of Israel, and as the Bible

says, the people "feared the king, for they saw that the wisdom of God was in him to do judgment."

His Parents

Solomon, who lived from 986 B.C. to 933 B.C., became king of Israel when he was about twelve years old. He was the son of David, the first great Hebrew king, and David's much-loved wife, Bathsheba. Solomon was not the oldest of David's sons, but he was the one chosen by his father to succeed him.

How He Won His Wisdom

Young as he was when he came to the throne, Solomon showed what a worthy successor he was to his father from the beginning.

The Bible gives an account of how he acquired his wisdom. One night, the story says, the Lord came to Solomon in a dream and asked him what he wished above all. Solomon answered:

"O Lord my God, thou hast made thy servant king instead of David my father, and I am but a little child: I know not how to go out or come in. . . . Give therefore thy servant an understanding heart to judge thy people, that I may discern between good and bad."

The Lord was very pleased that Solomon had not asked for riches or a long life or revenge on his enemies, and He answered him:

"Behold, I have done according to thy words: lo, I have given thee a wise and an understanding heart: so that there was none like thee before thee, neither after thee shall any arise like unto thee. And I have also given thee that which thou hast not asked, both riches and honour, so that there shall not be any among kings like unto thee all thy days."

His Achievements

Everything that the Lord promised Solomon came true in historical reality. The young ruler soon won the respect and love of his people and unified the country as it had not been unified before. He married the daughter of a Pharaoh of Egypt and so brought about friendly relations with that country. Gradually, he won the friendship of other neighboring countries and built up a flourishing trade with them.

He used the riches his father had left him so wisely, he encouraged trade so successfully, he handled taxation so thoughtfully, that Israel became wealthy as it had never been before. Solomon could build splendid palaces, court buildings, and cities.

Being wise, he avoided war, but he kept a large standing army at all times, with hundreds of armed chariots and thousands of horses. The Bible says that he had forty thousand stalls for horses.

The Temple

One of the great accomplishments of Solomon's reign was his building of a temple for the Lord in Jerusalem, his capital city. This was something his father, David, had never been able to finish because of the many wars during his reign.

Solomon planned a temple as large and beautiful as possible. He had a trading agreement with the wealthy King Hiram of Tyre. From Hiram he ordered and obtained rare woods, cedar, and fir, gold, ivory, and other precious things. Solomon also ordered fine and costly stone from distant regions. Then he set all the most skilled workmen of the kingdom to building the temple. The wood and the stone of the pillars, walls, and roof were carved with cherubim and palm trees. Then the roof, the floors, and many of the walls were overlaid with gold.

Seven years were spent in the building of the temple, and then it was furnished as richly as it had been built. Every article installed in it was of gold, silver, or finest wrought brass. Completed, the temple was the pride of Israel and remained so for four hundred years, until its destruction by the Babylonian king Nebuchadnezzar when he besieged and conquered Jerusalem in 586 B.C.

Solomon and the Queen of Sheba

The fame of Solomon, both for his wisdom and wealth, brought many visitors from other countries to Jerusalem to meet him. The Bible tells of the visit of the Queen of Sheba. Just what country she actually ruled over is not clear. The legends of the Arabs call her Balkis, queen of Saba.

The Bible goes into great detail about the splendid retinue that accom-

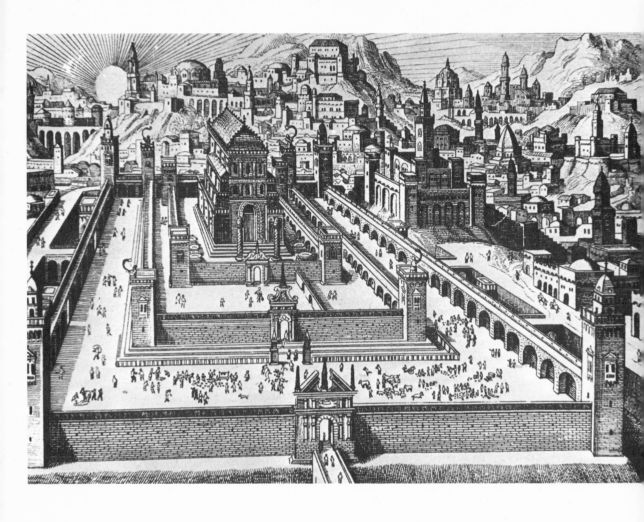

panied her to Jerusalem. Along with her ministers, advisors, handmaidens, servants, and so on, she had a great train of camels, laden with gold, precious stones, and rare spices.

The queen had come to see if Solomon was as wise as reported and had questions to ask him to test his wisdom. Solomon answered all her questions so easily and well that the queen was dazzled.

"Happy are thy men," she told him, "happy are these thy servants which stand continually before thee and that hear thy wisdom." Then, before leaving Jerusalem and returning to her own country, she gave him rich gifts from the gold, gems, and spices that she had brought with her.

Another story about Solomon and the Queen of Sheba (this one is not in the Bible) records that the queen was so impressed by the wise king that she became his wife and bore him a son who later became the founder of the Abyssinian dynasty.

Solomon's Downfall

After years of ruling with wisdom and good judgment, Solomon gradually began to grow careless. He had, as the custom was, many wives, and many of them were from neighboring countries where other gods than the Lord of Israel were worshiped. At first, Solomon insisted that such wives give up their worship of idols after marrying him, but through the years he became less firm about this requirement. He allowed temples to be built to the gods of his foreign wives. Then, every so often, Solomon began yielding to the urgings of one or another of his wives and taking part in the worship of their gods himself.

As news of this spread through the kingdom, there was first dismay, then growing anger. There were revolts and uprisings. The country that had been so united at the beginning of Solomon's reign began to be divided.

According to the Bible, the prophet Ahijah warned Solomon of the Lord's displeasure at his behavior and of what the Lord's punishment would be. The Israelites would be divided into twelve tribes again, and ten of them would be taken from Solomon's rule and given to a brave and devout young man named Jeroboam. Only one tribe and the city of Jerusalem would be left to Solomon and Solomon's son.

History records that this was what happened after Solomon's death, at the age of fifty-three. Ten tribes seceded from the kingdom over which Solomon had ruled, and Rehoboam, Solomon's son, who became king after his death, was unable to prevent those tribes from becoming a separate kingdom of Israel, leaving him only Jerusalem and Judah.

The Ten Lost Tribes

Those ten tribes of Jews who set up a separate kingdom ultimately became a legend themselves. Their kingdom lasted two hundred years but then, in 722 B.C., they were conquered by Sargon of Assyria and forced to leave their homeland. Twenty-seven thousand Jews were dispersed through the Assyrian Empire at that time, and what finally became of them is one of the puzzles of history.

Through the centuries, scholars, explorers, and men of every faith and nationality have offered different theories about the Ten Lost Tribes. Because Jewish monuments have been found in China, one theory says that the ten tribes went there. Other clues trace them to India. Some students once believed that they had found proof that the Anglo-Saxons were really descendants of the lost tribes, and another school of thought held for many years that the American Indians were the descendants of the vanished people.

Today, most historians believe that the ten tribes were simply absorbed into the various nations where they settled after leaving Israel and were never "lost" as a group, as legend insisted for so many centuries.

Solomon's Glory

The downfall of Solomon's kingdom makes a sad ending to his story but can never dim the splendor that shines over the years when he was in his glory, the wisest and one of the richest of kings, ruler of a land that was peaceful, prosperous, and God-fearing.

Legends About Solomon

Through the centuries, the Jewish people created and preserved many legends about their most splendid king.

One of these legends tells of a magic ring that Solomon had. When he wore this ring, he could understand the language of every bird and beast and living thing.

The story of this ring gave rise to other stories. One story concerned a friend of Solomon's who visited him every year and was always given a gift by the king when he departed. One year, when Solomon asked his friend what sort of gift he would like, the friend said that he would like most of all to understand the speech of animals as Solomon did.

The king was dismayed, not, he told his friend, because he did not wish to please him but because if he gave him the magic power he wished he must never tell a living soul that he had it or he would die instantly. The friend promised that he would never breathe a word about it if the king would just give him the power. At last Solomon consented. He touched his friend with the magic ring, and the friend departed for his home.

The friend, being a countryman, was delighted with his new power. When he got to his farm, he could hear the conversations of his ox and his donkey, his horse, his dog, and his chickens, and everything that the animals said entertained and amused him. But his wife grew curious as to what her husband was laughing at so much of the time. When he tried to put her off with lame excuses, she grew angry. At last she told him that unless he told her what was so funny she would leave him.

The man loved his wife very much. He thought that he might as well be dead as have her leave him, and so he promised he would tell her. First though, he went out into the barnyard for a last look at the fields, the sky, and the whole beautiful world he would soon be leaving. In the barnyard, he heard his dog telling the rooster what a fool his master was, condemning himself to death just to gratify a woman's curiosity. Surely, the dog said, the man has little faith in his wife's love if he thinks she would rather see him dead than have her curiosity unsatisfied.

The man came to his senses. He went into his house and asked his wife if she would rather see him dead than never know why he laughed. The woman, as it happened, loved the man as dearly as he loved her. When she realized that it was a life-or-death secret that her husband kept, she told him to keep the secret. Her love was stronger than her curiosity. So the man kept his magic power to understand animals—and also his wife and his life.

According to legend, Solomon loved horses and horse racing. He had a great hippodrome built in Jerusalem where the beautiful horses that he kept in the royal stables were raced once a month for the entertainment of the people.

He was also very fond of chess and played often with his chamberlain, Benaiah—whom he generally worsted.

Another legend tells of Solomon's adventures with Asmodeus, king of the demons. During the building of the temple, the workers came to Solomon and told him that they had a huge rock they found impossible to cut. Every method failed.

Solomon remembered a magic stone called a shamir, which could cut through any substance instantly. Unfortunately, only Asmodeus knew where this magic stone was hidden. So Solomon gave his chamberlain, Benaiah, the task of finding Asmodeus and winning the secret from him.

After many difficulties, Benaiah found the demon king and managed to capture him and learn the secret. He found the shamir, as directed, in the nest of a moor hen, and returned with it to Solomon. Solomon gave it to the builders, and their problem was solved.

But Asmodeus, angry at having been tricked, soon appeared and, in his turn, tricked Solomon into removing his magic ring for a moment. When Asmodeus had the magic ring on his own finger he transformed himself into a semblance of Solomon and then drove Solomon out of Jerusalem.

For months, Solomon wandered about the countryside, a poor beggar. At last he managed to get a job in the kitchen of a rich nobleman. One day, the nobleman's beautiful daughter, Naamah, saw him and fell in love with him. Solomon was soon in love with her also but when Naamah's father discovered his daughter's romance he was very angry. He banished both Naamah and Solomon from his lands.

Solomon and the maiden made their way to the seashore. There they met a fisherman, and since they were hungry they bought a fish that he had just caught. Naamah slit the fish, preparing it for the pan, and there in the fish's stomach was Solomon's magic ring. Solomon could only guess at how it had arrived there—Asmodeus must have lost it somehow—but with it on his finger again, his misfortunes were over.

He returned to Jerusalem with Naamah. With a flick of his hand, he changed Asmodeus back into the demon that he really was and again took over the rule of his country with Naamah as his queen.

Legend gives lavish descriptions of Solomon's throne. It was all of gold, encrusted with jewels, and six steps led up to it. At either end of each step was a lion and an eagle. Back of the throne were seventy golden chairs for the judges and advisors who made up his council, or Sanhedrin. Seated amidst this magnificence Solomon greeted all who sought him with the same quiet courtesy. And the poorest in his kingdom as well as the richest could benefit from the gift he had asked for—"an understanding heart."

PART SIX

KINGS FAMED
FOR THEIR BUILDING

In Xanadu did Kubla Khan
  A stately pleasure dome decree. . . .
    Kubla Khan, SAMUEL COLERIDGE (1772–1834)

Minos

Nebuchadnezzar

Louis XIV

23

Minos

The Minotaur and the Labyrinth

ACCORDING TO GREEK LEGEND, Minos was a king of the island of Crete in ancient days. He owned a terrifying beast, a creature with the head of a man and the body of a bull, which was called the Minotaur. This creature was so dangerous and destructive that King Minos had his state architect, Daedalus, design and build a very special sort of enclosure for it, from which escape was impossible. What Daedalus designed was a building composed of twisting halls, blind alleys, and false turnings so cleverly arranged that one could wander endlessly within the building without ever finding an exit. This maze was called the labyrinth and became famous throughout the world.

A terrible rite became connected with the Minotaur in this labyrinth. This rite was the consequence of a visit made by King Minos' only son to the city of Athens in Greece. While the lad was in Athens he was accidentally killed. In rage and revenge, Minos led his army in an attack on Athens. He captured the city and then declared he would destroy it unless every nine years he was sent a tribute of seven maidens and seven youths. The Athenians agreed to pay this price to save their city. Every nine years after that, when the Athenians sent seven youths and seven maidens who had been selected to Crete, Minos drove them into the labyrinth, to be devoured by the Minotaur.

This awful periodic sacrifice of Athenian youth went on for many years before the Athenian hero, Theseus, brought an end to the horror.

Theseus

One of the great heroes of Greek mythology, Theseus was equal, and in some ways almost superior, to Hercules. He had many adventures throughout his life, but his adventure with the Minotaur was one of the earliest.

Theseus was the son of the Athenian king Aegeus, but he had been raised far from the city by his mother and did not know of his royal inheritance until he was almost grown. Then, by rolling away a great stone that concealed a sword and a pair of shoes his father had hidden before the boy's birth, Theseus proved to his mother that he was ready to claim his rightful place in the world. He set off for Athens to meet his father and had many exciting experiences on the way, challenging and defeating many of the highwaymen and monsters who had made traveling a nightmare in that area for many years.

The news of his exploits went ahead of him so that he was already a hero when he arrived in Athens. His father, not knowing the young man was his son, was inclined to be jealous of him. The sorceress Medea, who did know who the new hero was, advised the king to poison the young man. Then Theseus drew his sword to make himself known to his father. His father recognized the weapon and welcomed his son with joy.

But Theseus had arrived in Athens in the very year and month that the seven youths and seven maidens were due to be sent to King Minos as tribute. He saw the grief of the citizens as they reluctantly began choosing those to be sent. Then he stepped forward and volunteered to be one of the number.

All Athens admired the king's son for this brave offer, and Theseus told no one but his father that he planned to kill the Minotaur if he could. The ship that would carry him and the other young people to Crete was fitted with black sails to signify its tragic mission. Theseus promised his father that if he was successful in killing the Minotaur, he would lower the black sails and raise white ones when he voyaged back so that his father would know well in advance that he had survived the ordeal.

So Theseus and the thirteen youths and maidens sailed for Crete. When they arrived at the island, they were paraded past King Minos and his court. Ariadne, the daughter of King Minos, saw Theseus and fell in love with him at first sight. Unable to bear the thought of him being killed by the Minotaur, Ariadne went to Daedalus, the man who had built the labyrinth, and asked him to tell her some way by which a person could escape from it.

Daedalus gave the maiden a clue, and she hurried to Theseus. She told him that she would help him get out of the labyrinth if he would take her back to

Athens with him afterward and marry her. Ariadne was a beautiful and charming maiden. It was not hard for Theseus to agree to her request. Then Ariadne gave him a ball of twine and told him to fasten one end at the inside of the door as he went into the labyrinth and unwind the string as he proceeded through its halls.

The time came for Theseus to enter the labyrinth—the first of the group. He took the ball of twine and did as Ariadne had told him, unwinding the twine as he went farther and deeper into the maze.

At last he came to the Minotaur. The terrifying creature was asleep. Theseus fell upon it, pinning it to the ground. Then he battered the monster to death with his hands. All alone and unarmed, he destroyed the beast which had caused so much pain and sorrow to the Athenians for years.

The deed done, he picked up the ball from the floor where he had dropped it and followed the unwound twine back to the door of the Labyrinth.

There was rejoicing among the youths and maidens who were waiting when they saw him. Theseus took Ariadne's hand, and then they all fled to the ship to return to Athens.

Two different stories are told as to what happened on the return voyage. One legend says that the ship put in at the island of Naxos for some repairs, that Ariadne fell asleep on the island, and that Theseus deserted her, returning to the ship and sailing away without her. Later she was found and comforted by the god Dionysus.

The other legend, which does more credit to Theseus, tells that Ariadne was seasick on the voyage. The ship was put in at Naxos so that she could rest a while on land. While she was resting, Theseus went back to the ship to make some small repairs. A storm blew up, carried him out to sea, and kept him there a long time. When he was finally able to return to the island he found that Ariadne had died, and he was very grieved.

Both versions agree, however, that for one reason or another, Theseus forgot to lower the black sails of the ship and to raise white ones as he approached Athens. His father, Aegeus, watching from a cliff, saw the black-sailed vessel approaching and concluded that his son had been killed by the Minotaur. In his grief, the king flung himself into the sea and was drowned. The sea where he perished has been called the Aegean Sea ever afterwards.

Theseus felt great grief and remorse when he landed and learned the result of his forgetfulness. But with his father dead, he was now king of Athens and

had to turn his attention to governing. He showed himself a wise and un-selfish king, making Athens a democracy and keeping no royal power for himself. Under his guidance, Athens became the happiest and most prosperous city in the world, and Theseus, as eager for adventure as always, went on to further heroic deeds.

Minos and Daedalus

When King Minos learned that Theseus had slain the Minotaur, found his way out of the labyrinth, and then escaped with Ariadne and the other Athenian young people, he was sure that Daedalus must have helped him. Only Daedalus would know a way to escape the labyrinthine maze. Angered by what seemed like treason, Minos imprisoned Daedalus in the labyrinth, which he had built, and with him, his son, Icarus.

Daedalus had no ball of thread such as he had given to Ariadne for Theseus, and soon he realized what an insoluble maze he had designed. He could find no way out for himself and his son. But he was a brilliant inventor and soon had an inspiration. If they could not get out on foot, perhaps they could fly to freedom.

Daedalus fashioned a pair of wings for himself and another pair for Icarus. He affixed them to their backs. Then, just before they took off through an opening in the roof of the labyrinth Daedalus gave his son a warning. He told him that after they were outside, the boy should fly a middle course over the sea. He cautioned him that if he tried to fly too high the sun would melt the glue of his wings, and they would drop off.

But as the father and son soared up and out of the labyrinth and then out over the blue sea, young Icarus became intoxicated with the joy of flight. He flew higher and higher, paying no heed to his father's cries. Nearer and nearer to the sun he rose. And then just what his father had predicted came to pass. The heat of the sun melted the glue of his wings. They dropped from him, and the boy fell like a plummet into the sea. Sadly, Daedalus saw him vanish and then flew slowly on to Sicily where he was received kindly by the king of that island.

Minos, really angry now as all of his prisoners seemed to escape him, thought of a cunning plan to trap Daedalus. He had it proclaimed everywhere that he would offer a great reward to anyone who could pass a thread through a very intricately spiraled shell. Daedalus heard of the offer and determined to accomplish the task. He bored a small hole in the closed end of the shell, then fastened a thread to an ant. He put the ant into the hole, after which he closed up the hole. When the ant emerged at last from the lip of the shell, the thread attached to it was running through all the twists and spirals inside the shell.

"Only Daedalus could think of that," said Minos when he heard of the solution. He hurried to Sicily to seize the inventor and architect. But the king of Sicily refused to surrender Daedalus. There was some flashing of swords, and in the struggle Minos was killed.

The Legend of Minos' Parentage

According to legend, Minos was a son of Zeus, chief of the gods, and a beautiful mortal maiden named Europa. Europa was a daughter of the king of Sidon, one of the Greek cities on the coast of Asia Minor. Zeus saw her gathering flowers in a meadow and thought she was so desirable that he changed himself into the shape of a bull to abduct her. He made himself such a handsome and gentle bull that when he knelt before the maiden, Europa willingly climbed on his back. Then the magic bull leaped up and raced with the maiden on his back to the seashore. There he rose into the air and flew over the waves to the island of Crete. When they arrived at the island, the magic bull revealed himself as Zeus. He told Europa that he had brought her to the island where his mother had sheltered him in a cave when he was an infant.

Europa had three sons by Zeus, of whom Minos was one. When Minos grew up and became ruler of Crete, he made Crete into a great sea power, trading with all the lands to the north, south, and east. In spite of the story about his harsh treatment of Athenian young people, he was supposed to be a very wise king. He was considered a lawgiver of such fine judgment that after his death he was made one of the judges of the underworld, where souls went after death to find either eternal punishment or everlasting bliss.

The Real King Minos as Discovered by Archaeologists

For centuries, the stories about Minos, his kingdom and his labyrinth,

were considered nothing more than myths, told and retold by Greek writers but having no foundation in fact. Then, around the beginning of the twentieth century, archaeologists following the lead of Heinrich Schliemann, who had dug down to find the original city of Troy in Asia Minor, began to dig in Crete.

Beneath the soil and rock of the deserted countryside, these scientists began to find evidence of a once brilliant civilization. Sir Arthur Evans, digging near Knossos, unearthed the foundations, walls, and staircases of what had plainly been a splendid palace. Furniture, art work, beautiful frescoes, household tools, and implements were found also.

To fix a date for the years when the palace had been in use, the actual home of rulers of Crete, Sir Arthur studied the pottery found in the excavations. Comparing it to pottery found in Egypt, for which dates were known, Evans and other scholars made an amazing discovery. The civilization on Crete dated back two thousand years before the time of Homer. Its beginnings were, it seems, around 3000 B.C.

The discovery of the buried palace and the realization of its age gave a new reality to Homeric stories about King Minos. The vanished civilization unearthed in Crete was named the Minoan civilization because it now seemed quite probable that a King Minos *had* ruled in Crete, sometime between 2500 and 1200 B.C., when the kingdom was most flourishing. During those remote centuries, a time to which scholars had assigned western civilization only to Mesopotamia and Egypt, Crete was a rich sea power, trading with Egypt and Asia Minor, influencing and being influenced by Egyptian art and customs.

What brought this rich Cretan civilization to a sudden end, two hundred years and more before Homer's time and the beginnings of Greek civilization, no one knows for sure. Perhaps it was an attack by enemies who leveled the palace and all the buildings around it. Perhaps it was an earthquake, since earthquakes are not uncommon in Crete.

The Real Labyrinth

No actual labyrinth has been discovered in connection with the palace at Knossos, but the palace itself is full of twisting halls and blind alleys and rooms leading from one to another, very like a maze. It is considered possible that the palace may have been called *labyrinthose* by the ancients, and this, combined with stories about its mazelike construction, gave rise to the story about a labyrinth with a monster in it.

The story of the labyrinth might also have been inspired by a cave, of which there are many in Crete. It is known that ages ago, during the time of the Minoan civilization, the king had to descend periodically into one of the larger caves to perform certain religious duties.

The Real Minotaur

There was, of course, never any real Minotaur—half man, half bull. But frescoes on the walls of the palace of Knossos and drawings on pottery and on small seals and coins make it clear that the bull played an important part in the ancient Cretan religion.

There are also frescoes that show young men and women engaged in a strange and curious sport which can only be described as bull-leaping. A young man stands before a bull charging with lowered horns. When the bull comes close enough, the youth grasps the horns, somersaults up and over the bull's head onto its back, then up and over again backward to alight on the ground.

These pictured scenes of what seems like a well-nigh incredible acrobatic feat may explain the myth of the Minotaur. Perhaps captives, from the mainland of Greece, were required to perfect this skill of bull-leaping and then perform in the heart of the mazelike palace for the entertainment of the nobles of the Minoan court. The danger and the number of deaths involved might well have given rise to a legend about a bull-like monster that the king of Crete fed with human victims.

24
Nebuchadnezzar

THIS BABYLONIAN KING of ancient times is sometimes remembered for what seems like absurd behavior. People say that he went out in the fields and ate grass.

It is true, according to the Bible, that King Nebuchadnezzar did suffer a spell of insanity near the end of his life. While deranged, he imagined that he was an animal and ate grass as cattle do. But this bizarre episode is only part of the story of Nebuchadnezzar, a king who distinguished himself in various ways—as warrior, conqueror, and destroyer—and as a builder as well.

When He Lived

Almost fifteen centuries had passed since Hammurabi had first brought Babylon to its days of glory. The city had been conquered again and again and almost destroyed by the Assyrians, under Sennacherib, when they were at the height of their power. And then, toward the end of the seventh century B.C., Nebuchadnezzar's father managed to win Babylonian independence and establish a Chaldean or New Babylonian Empire.

As a youth, Nebuchadnezzar led his father's armies against the Egyptians who had moved in on Syria and Palestine and drove them back into Egypt. And then, in 605 B.C., he became king, to rule until 562 B.C.

The Sack of Jerusalem

Not long after he became king, Nebuchadnezzar undertook to subdue the rebellious activities of the Hebrew kingdom in Judah. Twice he laid siege to Jerusalem, the city that David had captured from the Philistines and that Solomon had made into a splendid capital. The first time Nebuchadnezzar

was victorious and took the king of Judah back to Babylonia with him as a prisoner, putting a puppet king on the throne of Judah. Then rebellion broke out again in 586 B.C., and Nebuchadnezzar swept down on the city once more.

This time when he won the city he showed no mercy but destroyed it almost entirely, leaving Solomon's temple in ruins. And this time when he returned to Babylonia, he took with him not only the king but thousands of other Jews, among them nobles, princes, and the flower of Jewish youth. The period of almost fifty years that these Jews were prisoners in Babylonia is known to history as the Babylonian captivity.

The Young Men in the Fiery Furnace

Nebuchadnezzar's treatment of his Jewish prisoners was not especially harsh or cruel. In fact, he seems to have been somewhat fascinated by them and their unusual belief in one God who forebade them to worship any other god whatsoever. He gave three young Jews, who were called in the Babylonian language Shadrach, Meshach, and Abednego, positions of trust in his country. And the young Jewish noble and prophet Daniel, whose adventures are recorded in the Book of Daniel in the Bible, found favor in Nebuchadnezzar's eyes by his ability to interpret the king's dreams. (This was the same Daniel who was later cast into a lion's den, but it was one of Nebuchadnezzar's successors who tested Daniel's faith in the Lord of Israel in that extreme fashion. And it was for Nebuchadnezzar's grandson, Belshazzar, that Daniel interpreted the famous handwriting on the wall, "Mene, mene, tekel, upharsin," as a warning that the great empire of Babylonia would soon fall.)

During his reign Nebuchadnezzar was responsible for a test of the faith of his Jewish prisoners. He had a great golden image constructed and ordered all his people to bow down and worship it. The Jewish captives, obedient to their god's commandment that they should not bow down to any idols, refused to obey the order. The king's authorities singled out the three young men, Shadrach, Meshach, and Abednego, to be punished as examples.

Reluctantly, Nebuchadnezzar was forced to follow the letter of his own laws and order that the young men be burned to death in a fiery furnace. Guards led Shadrach, Meshach, and Abednego to the furnace where a fire had been built up to be seven times hotter than it usually was. The heat was

so intense, in fact, that the guards perished from it even as they threw the bound young men into the furnace mouth.

But the three young men rose to their feet in the midst of the blaze and then walked unharmed through the flames.

Astonished, Nebuchadnezzar went to the mouth of the furnace and summoned the young men to come out. After that, he declared his awe of the God of Israel who had protected them so miraculously.

Nebuchadnezzar's Madness

It was not long after the young men had survived the ordeal of the fiery furnace that Nebuchadnezzar had a curious dream. Daniel said it foretold that he would go mad, his heart being changed from a man's heart to a beast's. Within the year, according to the Bible, Daniel's prophecy was fulfilled. Nebuchadnezzar went mad, was driven from his palace, "and did eat grass as oxen, and his body was wet with the dew of heaven, till his hairs were grown like eagles' feathers, and his nails like birds' claws."

When Nebuchadnezzar finally recovered his senses, he repented his sins as Daniel had told him he must and praised and extolled the Israelite God.

The Hanging Gardens

Aside from his various concerns with his Jewish captives, Nebuchadnezzar engaged in other activities not recorded in the Bible.

A splendor-loving king, he started rebuilding Babylon as soon as he began his rule. He had fine new walls put up around the city. Lavish new buildings were erected and towered temples splashed with color. Most splendid of all was the great brick palace he had built for himself. Colored tiles paving the floors and walls made it a brilliant place. But the most unusual aspects of the palace were the terraced gardens he had put in against the palace walls.

The luxuriant foliage and bloom of the plants in these gardens, stepped up one above the other, made a sight so beautiful and unique that people called them the Hanging Gardens. The crowning touch of loveliness that these gardens added to a city already glittering with barbaric splendor caused people to call the Hanging Gardens of Babylon one of the Seven Wonders of the World.

Just as Daniel predicted for Nebuchadnezzar's grandson, the Babylonian Empire was soon to be destroyed. Only twenty years or so after Nebuchadnezzar's death, Cyrus the Great of Persia conquered Babylonia, and before long the brilliant city of Babylon was just another outpost in the Persian Empire.

But memories of its glories in Nebuchadnezzar's days lingered on. Two hundred years later, Alexander the Great, halting there, thought of making it his capital. And though sun, wind, and sand have ravaged the city through all the centuries since, and most of Nebuchadnezzar's towers are ruins, tourists can still see the outlines of the Hanging Gardens, once one of the Wonders of the World.

25
Louis XIV

Louis XIV was the Sun king, shining with a magnificence that dazzled not only France but all of Europe through the last half of the seventeenth century. The dream of this Louis, the fourteenth to rule France (the first was Louis the son of Charlemagne), was to be known as a brilliant military leader. What really won him his name of Sun King was the marvelous palace that he built at Versailles and the splendor of the court life that he encouraged there.

His Long Reign

Louis was born in 1638, the grandson of Henry IV of Navarre and the son of Louis XIII. Because he was only five years old when his father died and he succeeded to the throne, and because he lived until 1715, he was king for seventy-two years, an unusually long span of time. Of course he did not actually begin ruling at the age of five. His mother, Anne of Austria, who was appointed his regent, and her Prime Minister, Cardinal Mazarin, ran the country for several years. But Louis was considered of age when he was thirteen, which meant that he actually ruled for sixty-four years. He outlived his son and his grandson. His successor Louis XV, who succeeded him, was his great-grandson.

L'État, C'Est Moi

When Louis was still a very young boy, the citizens of Paris grew enraged by the way some of Anne of Austria's ministers cheated and swindled the public. Their wrath was so great that Anne thought it wise to take her young son and herself into hiding outside of Paris to escape harm. That may have been one of the reasons why Louis, when he took command, refused to rely completely on any minister and made himself familiar with the details of every department of government. Gradually, he made himself an absolute ruler who was subject to no checks or controls by anybody or any group.

"L'état, c'est moi," he said. "I am the state." Other European rulers whose authority was limited by parliaments and other elected or hereditary bodies looked at Louis XIV of France and were envious of his power.

Louis as a Warrior

War fascinated Louis from his earliest childhood. His favorite pastimes were playing with toy soldiers or waging mimic war with young friends. As soon as he was old enough, he rode out eagerly to command French forces in the field. France had a fine army, well drilled, well equipped and well generaled. As a result, the French forces had many victories, and Louis happily took the credit for them. Actually, he was not an especially talented military strategist, but his generals tactfully pretended to follow his advice or encouraged him to think their plans were his originally. And it all worked out very well for a long time. After a long campaign in Holland was finally successful in 1678, France became the most powerful country in Europe.

Many years later, when Louis was growing old, half of Europe united to form a league against him and his powerful country. In the battles that followed, French generals were not so successful as they had been. When they faced the English forces led by the Duke of Marlborough they knew real defeat. Some of France's possessions in America—Newfoundland, Acadia, and Hudson's Bay—were ceded to the English when the Peace of Utrecht was finally signed in 1713.

Louis had but two more years to live, and it seems that in those last years he regretted the hardships he had caused his countrymen in the past by his love of war and a conqueror's glory.

Versailles

All through the years when he was pursuing glory in battle, Louis was also creating the palace that would bring him his most enduring fame.

His father, Louis XIII, had built a hunting lodge not far from Paris near a tiny town called Versailles. In 1661, when Louis XIV was twenty-three, he

decided to use the lodge as the nucleus of a beautiful new palace which would reflect his love of everything spacious, elegant and symmetrical. He summoned France's finest architects, engineers and landscape gardeners and set them to work. (One of these architects was Jules Hardouin Mansart, a nephew of an earlier architect whose name was given to a special style of roof still in use today, the mansard roof.)

Millions of francs were poured into the creation of the palace at Versailles, and Louis spent more than twenty years perfecting it. Everything about it was splendid. There were dozens of great halls—a Galerie des Batailles, lined with huge paintings of French victories, Le Hall des Glaces, or great hall lined with mirrors, and most magnificent of all, the Throne Room with a silver throne. Living orange trees in silver tubs were placed at intervals all around this great room.

Sweeping staircases led from one floor to another. There were dozens of private suites, a private chapel, rooms beyond rooms beyond rooms. And everywhere there were great, high windows, for Louis loved the look of the outdoors and the feel of fresh breezes sweeping in.

Outside the palace, hundreds of acres were drained, filled, and landscaped. Formal gardens became great patterns of living color. Water was piped from one hundred miles away and a huge machine constructed to provide water pressure for dozens of splashing fountains. There were mazes, labyrinths, and formal walks with pieces of sculpture carefully placed to make the most of every vista.

The interior of the palace was furnished on the same lavish scale. Gold and silver brocade hung at the windows. Furniture was rich and elaborate, carved or inlaid with ivory or precious metals. Glass cabinets held exotic curios, and the walls were hung with paintings by the world's greatest masters.

Books and music also pleased Louis. Over the years he collected what was a very large library for the time, and he kept it open for everyone's use. Musicians in large enough numbers to make up a full symphony orchestra lived in the palace to provide daily musical entertainment.

Life at Versailles

In 1682, Louis moved the seat of his government from Paris to Versailles. This meant that literally thousands of his subjects were obliged to follow him, not just the chief nobility and government officials but everyone who based his hopes of success on being noticed by the great king.

Not everyone was pleased by the move away from Paris, but the palace at Versailles had become the showplace of Europe, and the great of every country flocked to visit it.

The days at Versailles passed in a glittering round of activities. Every day there was some sort of festivity. Every evening there was a ball, a concert, an opera, or a play. An elaborate ritual of courtesy and ceremony was observed at all times. This sort of court etiquette, for which Louis himself set the example, was widely imitated all over Europe as the ultimate in civilized behavior.

The wonder was that in spite of so much festivity, so many visitors, and so many courtiers vying for his notice Louis still managed to spend a good portion of every day working on matters of state, making decisions, and directing the policies of the nation. He also found time to go hunting almost every day, for he was an outdoorsman who enjoyed all kinds of energetic outdoor activity.

His Love Affairs

Louis was married to Marie Thérèse of Austria in 1660. He was fond of his wife but soon after his marriage embarked on the first of a series of love affairs that scandalized even his most tolerant subjects. His first favorite was Louise de la Vallière (a certain type of necklace is still called by her name). Next he fell in love with the Marquise de Montespan, who practiced black magic to keep his love. She was finally disgraced when it was revealed that she had taken part in a poisoning plot. Louis had still other loves, but at last he fell under the influence of a shrewd, intelligent, and pious woman, Madame de Maintenon, who devoted most of her energy to trying to reform him. Perhaps Louis was ready for such a change. After his queen, Marie Thérèse, died in 1683, Louis secretly married Madame de Maintenon. From then on, he became more concerned with religion, and life at Versailles became more austere.

His Harshness to Protestants

Louis' new concern with religion led him finally to undo the good work that his grandfather, Henry IV, had done to bring religious tolerance to France. He was a devout Roman Catholic himself and became even more so under Madame de Maintenon's influence. Easily roused to suspicion by any report about the activities of French Huguenots, or Protestants, he at last decided to take action against them. In 1685, he revoked the Edict of Nantes which Henry IV had signed almost a hundred years before. French Huguenots were no longer allowed to worship according to Protestant beliefs.

As a result there was a mass migration of Huguenots from France at the end of the seventeenth century, and France lost many hard-working and talented citizens to other lands. Many took the long voyage to America and settled in the New World, especially in the Carolina colonies, Pennsylvania, and New York.

The Great Men of France During His Reign

So many brilliant generals, admirals, writers, artists, and engineers lived during the reign of Louis XIV and were encouraged by him that his reign has been called the Golden Age of France. A few of the most famous writers were Corneille, Racine, and Molière. Some well-known painters were Claude Lorraine, Poussin, and LeBrun.

Louis' Character

Louis has been called proud, vain, selfish, and extravagant, and to a degree he was probably all of those. He was surrounded by flatterers from infancy, and only a miracle could have kept him from being somewhat arrogant. However, he was also a hard-working king, never skimping on the time he devoted to affairs of state. He was a man of great dignity, who rarely lost his temper. He loved children and encouraged Madame de Maintenon to found and supervise a school for the daughters of impoverished noblemen at St. Cyr, near Versailles. Later, the school at St. Cyr became a famous military academy, the West Point of France. He also loved his subjects, the people of France, and it was not he but his great-grandson, Louis XV, who paved the way for the French Revolution by his reckless disregard of the welfare of the country.

The End of the Parade

There have been kings—and many of them—since the time of Louis XIV. But even while Louis was alive, wielding his absolute authority, men were beginning to question a belief that had been general for thousands of years— that kings somehow had a divine right to rule them. Various revolutions, including America's, have since helped to destroy that belief almost everywhere in the world.

So Louis XIV, in his splendor and power, seems to stand almost at the end of a long procession, a parade of kings stretching back through the centuries. Some were good, some bad, some greedy, some wise, but all had some of the splendor and power that were Louis XIV's. And looking back at them from a distance, it is easy to see them as representing through the ages all the virtues and vices of mankind—on a truly kingly scale.

Chronology

ANCIENT TIMES

Midas (legendary) King of Phrygia (Asia Minor)
Minos (half-legendary, around 2000 B.C.) King of Crete
Hammurabi (1990 B.C. to 1913 B.C.) King of Babylon
Ikhnaton (1385 B.C. to 1358 B.C.) Pharaoh of Egypt
David (around 1000 B.C.) King of Judah
Solomon (about 986 B.C. to 933 B.C.) King of Israel and Judah
Ahab (about 900 B.C. to 853 B.C.) King of Israel
Nebuchadnezzar (620 B.C. ? to 562 B.C.) King of Babylon
Croesus (about 500 B.C.) King of Lydia (Asia Minor)
Alexander (356 B.C. to 323 B.C.) King of Macedonia
Mithridates (about 134 B.C. to 63 B.C.) King of Pontus (Asia Minor)
Nero (A.D. 37 to 68) Emperor of Rome

THE DARK AGES AND MEDIEVAL TIMES

Attila (around A.D. 400) King of the Huns
Arthur (around A.D. 500) Briton chieftain in northern England
Charlemagne (A.D. 742 to 814) King of the Franks
Harold Fairhair (around A.D. 850) King of Norway
Alfred (A.D. 849 to 899) King of England
Canute (A.D. 995 to 1035) King of England, Denmark, and Norway
William (A.D. 1027 to 1087) King of England, Duke of Normandy
Richard (A.D. 1157 to 1199) King of England

THE RENAISSANCE

Richard III (A.D. 1452 to 1485) King of England
Henry VIII (A.D. 1491 to 1547) King of England
Ivan (A.D. 1530 to 1584) Tsar of Russia
Henry IV (A.D. 1553 to 1610) King of France
Louis XIV (A.D. 1638 to 1715) King of France